"KENYA MATTERS"

Ralph Palmer 1955 - 1969

Copyright @ Ralph Palmer 2021
ISBN : 978-1-956017-31-1 - paperback
: 978-1-956017-32-8 - eBook

The right of Ralph Palmer to be identified as the author of this work has been asserted by him in accordance with the Copyright Design and Patents Acts 1988.

Published by Akis Investments
P.O. Box 47561 Nairobi 00100 Kenya. email: rainbowadd@yahoo.com

Cover Design by Ralph Palmer

"KENYA MATTERS"
Ralph Palmer 1955 - 1969

Second Edition.
Printed by English Press,P.O.Box 30127,Nairobi 00100,Kenya.
Email: mail@englishpress.com

This book is a work of non-fiction based on the life experiences and recollections of the author. In some limited cases the names and dates, places and sequences may have been changed, solely to protect the privacy of others. The author apologises for any omissions and will be pleased to make the appropriate acknowledgements in any future edition.

No part of this book may be reproduced or utilised in any form or by any means, electronic or mechanical, or by any information storage and retrieval system, without permission in writing from the publisher.

Final balloting before Independence on the strike of midnight, 12th December 1963

Dedication

To my dear wife Salma, my anchor in life.

Appreciation

Without the friendship of Peter Shiyukah much of this book would not have been written. We first met in Kitale District in 1962 and kept in touch; eventually, he arranged for my transfer from the Provincial Administration in Nakuru to the Ministry of Lands and Settlement Nairobi in 1966. Over the years we confided in each other and our humour enjoyed the state of the world when it was a more agreeable place; our philosophy, a more meaningful life.

Other titles by the same author
RAINBOW ADDICTION
NUKES WILD
DEADLINE
ROUGH JUSTICE
CODE ORANGE

Contents

Chapters

1,2, 3, Early planning.

4,5,6, Nyeri Area.

7,8, Meru, drive via Nanyuki.

9, Legislative Council Elections, Meru 1957.

10,11, Meru and Zanzibar Safari.

12,13, Machakos, 1961 Legislative Elections.

14,15, Nakuru, Kitale.

16, Kampala and Lodwar visits.

17,18, Baringo, Independence Elections 1963.

19, Independence.

20,21,22, Arrival Nairobi, Question-time in Parliament, Anecdotes and Future aspirations.

MAP OF EAST AFRICA

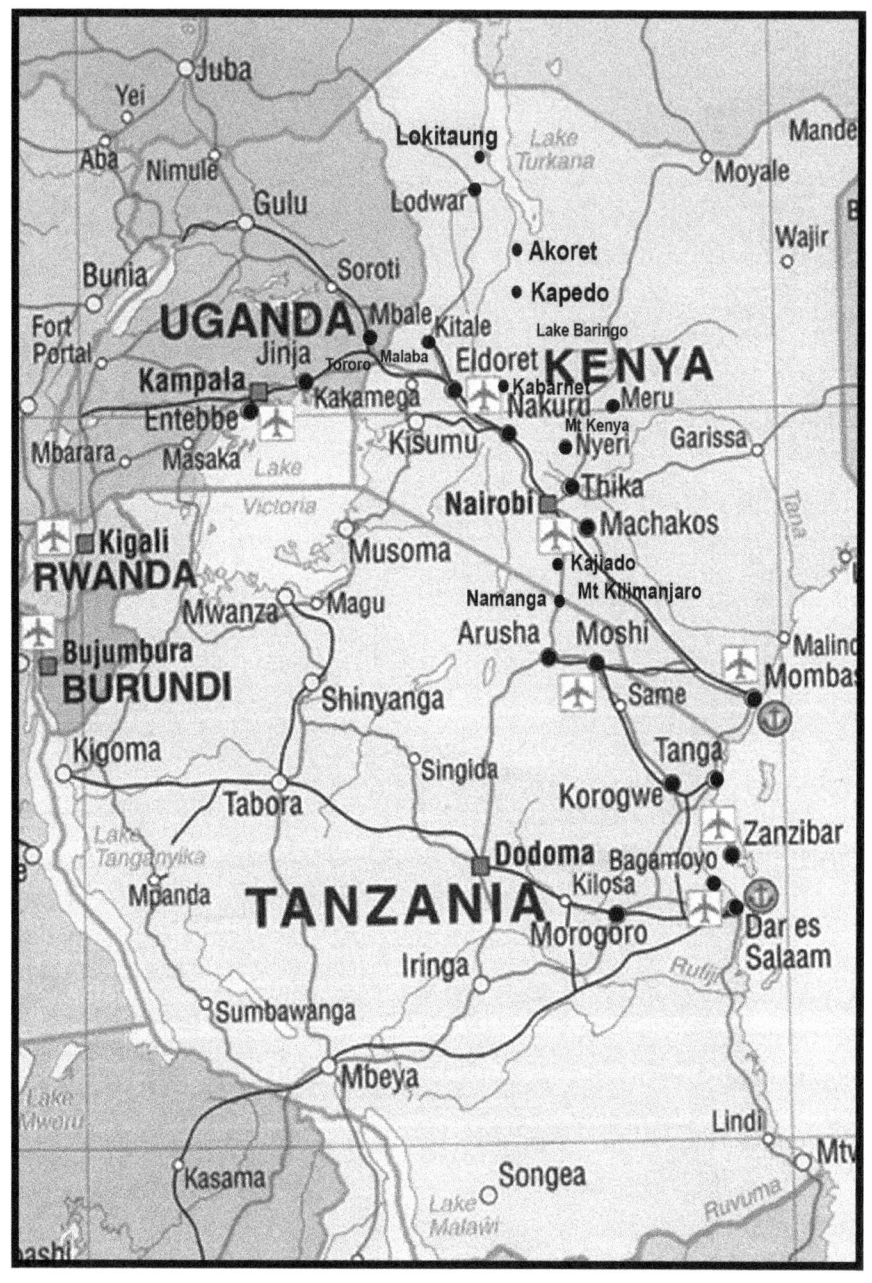

Prelude

My recollections of the past may well appear unusual, though in their time they were perfectly normal; I know, because I was there. Some characters I met rewarded me greatly; events were educational and eye opening.

This is a first-hand experience by the author and hearsay is only a small part of the text. A fictional Gulag about Kenya with mind-boggling figures and fanciful stories that don't add up is not my intention; this is a real sequence of events during my service with the Kenya Government, 1955 to 1969. One short period was recorded in diary form and used for reference; my election safari south of Lake Rudolf (Turkana) in the lead-up to Independence.

Some 50 years ago is what this book is all about, events in the Kenya Civil Service just before and just after Independence. With the passing of time I suspect my memory is somewhat sketchy, so I ask for your tolerance where omissions have slipped through the net to keep your enquiring minds busy. Since I am writing in the present about the past, I will on occasion compare the present with the past to air additional thinking shaped by time; please bear with me. To the personalities I may mention, I say thank you for having shaken my hand in friendship; you are part of the memories I now fondly recall.

Close encounter, Mombasa Road 1959

1

The British passport was a new idea when my father began his travels; decades would lapse before it was used on a junket to Spain for beer and chips. It first appeared on the scene as a printed document around 1915, and the gender inside the front cover has only changed once since its original issue, when Princess Elizabeth ascended the throne on alighting from 'Tree Tops' in Kenya.

The original idea of the passport really rests with Henry VIII, the guy who founded the British navy and chopped-off a few heads to solve his domestic problems. He issued letters patent for people to pass without let or hindrance some 500 years ago; on occasion the head of his messenger came back in a bag to teach Henry a lesson, though more often than not the letters patent prevailed. That's roughly the history of how the passport evolved to become the hassle of today, which has to be the fault of the British. But some of their better deeds to balance the ugly are football, tennis, cricket, golf and traffic lights, to mention a few of the many.

Rex Palmer was an adventurous soul intent on seeing the world after leaving Ashford Grammar, but a shortage of funds demanded a working event and not a luxury cruise. His father, my grandfather, was a chemist with a shop in Earls Barton, England, and when I was born my mother, with a threat from her mother-in-law, my father and everyone else for that matter, was told to name me after my grandfather and I would surely inherit his fortune. I was duly christened Ralph Palmer, like the name on the board over the shop, and surprise, surprise, his fortune then went to my uncle's side of the family.

When it was clear that no financial assistance for foreign travel would be forthcoming from the old man, my father chose an alternative to live out his dreams, an international company with overseas opportunities. After a short training period he set sail for Darwin in the Australian Northern Territories, in the employ of the Eastern Telegraph Company. Travel to distant lands was still considered risqué at that time. Cornwall in the southwest of England was the furthest distance to which the ordinary man could aspire, though over the centuries there were always exceptions, such as the free spirited pirates, buccaneers, freebooters, and of course the colonial era plunderers of our time, who settled in Kenya to develop the land. The East and Far East was any landmass east of Suez. The East India Company had to be India, and the Far East would start in the region of Burma and work its way towards Hong Kong, China, and stretch as far as Japan and the Philippines before it became the West Coast of America. Greenwich was the centre of the universe from which all measurements stemmed. 1923 was the year young Rex embarked for the Far East as a Morse-key-operator with high speed typing skills on cumbersome machines; he was nineteen at the time. Printed messages were pasted onto telegram forms from distant points in the Empire, but to send such details was an expensive affair when charged by the word. So to counter the cost, international companies used five letter codes to form whole sentences.

Strange though it may seem, similar methods were demonstrated to me when I first started work at Dodwell and Company on the 1st January 1951. My hired dinner jacket from the night before had been changed to a working-day suit with the strains of Auld Lang Syne still ringing in my ears. To decipher 5-letter codes on New Year's Day was my introduction to the business world; the Scots celebrated and the English sweated before they got wise and took the day off, to relax like the Scots.

In the distant days of my father, communications were dispatched thousands of miles by submarine cables using the Morse code, 'dots and dashes' to convey the message. It was then the turn of the office messenger to jump on his bike and deliver the telegram, deemed as an old fashioned door to door service. Deaths, marriages and births used this facility as a matter of course, and the dreaded telegrams in World War 1 and WW2 were the worst type of message one could expect; 'killed in action' etc…

A cargo ship in the 1920s took about 6 weeks from Southampton to Singapore depending on the ports of call, and the more direct passenger liner took a lesser time. Aeroplanes and airlines were still in their formative stages, and why would anyone risk their lives in the air when there was a more leisurely society of cabin trunks with snap open locks and wooden bindings; uniformed porters were also on hand to handle such luggage with no weight restrictions. The P & O (Peninsular and Oriental Steamship Company) was thriving. These were the years of 'no hassle' and my parents cherished such memories. As a boy, I recall my father showing me his first driving licence bought at the post office, no test required; how leisurely can you get? In fact, the first driving tests for mechanised transport such as motor vehicles, motorcycles and the charabanc were introduced on 26th March 1934; the day I was born, no less. My arrival on the scene had nothing to do with such impositions in England, though it's still quite possible to obtain a licence in Kenya without a test; but the procedure challenges.

Alice and Rex, my mother and father to be, first met in Darwin Australia; a place where the sand and thicket is 'king' and the likes of 'Crocodile Dundee' use bushman's skills. Chinese pearl divers harvested the seas and strangers to the area innovated for themselves. Alice was teaching at the local school and Rex was relaying marine-cable traffic. The date on a silver cigarette case presented to him by the 'Darwin Gun Club' indicates the year to be 1925; Rex was 21 years old at that time. Subsequently they married in Singapore and honeymooned in Java after a wedding reception at 'Raffles Hotel', a world heritage site today. As an errant son, I turned up at that same hotel in 1978 some 53 years later, to pay my respects by potting the black in the snooker room where my father used to play; his ghost was surely in the rafters. Rex returned to England and Alice went back to her parents' in Queensland to wind-up her affairs before following. After a difficult spell with the in-laws in England they moved to Raglan Court, Empire Way, opposite Wembley stadium, the traditional home of football. My brother was born in 1932 and I appeared on the scene in '34. In those days the midwife came home to deliver the brat; plenty of hot water, a white enamel basin, and the bawling infant filled the room.

My father's next overseas posting involved a short boat trip to Gibraltar in 1942, but a German U-Boat changed the course of our lives when it sank the ship with a company man on his way to Ascension Island. Luckily for us, he was washed ashore in Gibraltar to fill my father's posting ahead of schedule; my father then stepped ashore in George Town, Ascension Island, to take his place a few months later.

In November 1944, my mother Alice, my brother John and I were squeezed into a taxi at the Adelphi Hotel bound for the Liverpool docks. The famous clock-tower on the wharf struck midnight as we arrived, and fortunately for us the wintry sky afforded protection from Luftwaffe bombing, which was almost non-existent since the 'D' day landings in Europe. To pause and admire the view from the top of the gangplank was just not there; we were quickly bundled below for a first-time cabin experience. It was different, it was new, it was something else entirely; bunk beds, heavy brass-ringed portholes and a stainless steel washbasin was to be our home for the next 2 weeks.

Our departure from Liverpool docks was timed to rendezvous with a convoy of merchant ships escorted by a flotilla of Royal Navy frigates, our numbers were to be our protection against marauding U-Boats as we sailed towards Gibraltar. Seas south of Ireland and the Bay of Biscay are some of the most turbulent waters in the world when a gale force wind is blowing, much like the prevailing conditions the following morning. We awoke to the thrill of pitching and rolling, creaking protests from wooden interiors and groans from straining hull plates, all magic to our young ears. At breakfast the chairs were attached to the floor by a thin brass chain under the seats, and the flaps on the table edges were locked in an upright position to prevent the china from crashing to the floor. But to cap it all, the stewards were the 'stars' of the show as they faultlessly delivered the food to challenge the topsy-turvy.

Up on deck after breakfast, we kids forced our way through the wind to grab the ship's side-rails as our bows stood still like a plane in touchdown mode, before they plunged into a watery trough, to be lifted again. We hung on for dear life and gripped the rails in terror, to be cooled by the sea in body and mind. Abreast of us the escort vessels danced from out of sight to a silhouette on the skyline; how much more excitement can you get at the age of ten? Alice was not too pleased with our soaking wet clothes so early on in the day, though we boys were over the moon, our mischief repaid beyond belief.

Two days later we parted company with the lead-ships as they turned towards the Mediterranean with supplies for General Montgomery, who was directing the 8th army in the Libyan desert. On changing course, a flashing light from an escort vessel signalled a good-luck message, radio silence duly observed. Our ship the "S.S. Themistocles" of the Shaw Saville Line then struck out on her own to complete the voyage from Liverpool to Ascension in 14 days. All told, our family stayed on the Island from November 1944 to the end of '46, where we celebrated Victory Europe and Victory Japan with fireworks supplied by the American forces. During the Ascension adventure, we boys enjoyed the nearest thing to heaven on earth as we rode on the backs of green sea turtles and swam with the fish.

2

The family thirst for overseas travel came to the fore when my brother John left school and joined Cable & Wireless; the same company in which my father was working in '48 when he died in Kingston Town, Jamaica, but a short walk from the future house of Bob Marley. At the tender age of 45 he had succumbed to an illness whilst installing cable lines in the Turks and Caicos Islands. A time in history when penicillin had yet to become a worldwide healer.

After Ascension Island, long leave came into play yet again and my parents used the extra time to find a boarding school for us boys; we had to catch up on our learning after the Ascension holiday. I was twelve and John was fourteen by then, so it wasn't too difficult to leave us behind when they sailed off to the Turks and Caicos Islands, my father's next and final posting. Home leaves always varied in length according to the tour of duty and a ship was the standard mode of travel; step ashore and the leave began. A first class cabin was the norm, as indeed it was in the Colonial Service before air travel switched in. Our family had always been on the move, which now begged the question to realise my travelling dreams when I left school?

My first stop had been the Royal Air Force in 1952 followed by a stint at Dodwells, to continue my overseas training in the Baltic Exchange building at 24 St Mary Axe, EC3. No. 24 today is a brand-new London landmark, affectionately called the 'Gherkin' due its shape; designed and built by the French in 2004 it replaced the original Exchange bombed by the I.R.A., who were out to teach the Brits a lesson.

But well before that bombing, I had the honour to meet Sir Winston Churchill on the steps of 'our' offices so to speak; the Baltic Exchange that housed the 'Lutine Bell', tolled when a vessel was lost at sea. Our encounter, Winston and I, well... it wasn't really that personal, though it was quite by chance and easier than I expected. I merely walked up the steps towards this living legend, homburged and smoking a giant cigar. He politely took hold of my proffered hand and no words were exchanged; I was but a fly in the ointment to him and he was the Prime Minister of England. I was barely given a second glance from the tired chubby face he wore that day as he posed for the press, not with me I hasten to add, a few others only were gawping. As the cheeky young boy who had dared to do what he had to do on the spur of the moment, my spirits were high for the rest of the day. Yes, I washed the hand that shook the hand before I went to bed that night, only to recall the Yalta Conference when that very same person had shaken the hand of Stalin, to prove there is no shame if you wish to sup with the devil. In these modern times, politicians as bold as brass shake hands with the devil and look him straight in the eye as an equal, and the 'shorter the handle' to do the supping, the more comfortable they feel.

Soon after that episode with Churchill, I left Dodwell and the offices in the Baltic Exchange for them to follow me out to

Kenya many years later, to trade under the name of Deacons. They had opened a shop next door to Alibhai Shariff in Kimathi Street. The name 'Deacons' was cleverly coined from the words Dodwell, East Africa, Company, Nairobi. It was controlled by the very same head-office where I had wasted a couple of years hanging on for an overseas job. Fortunately for my future, I was also studying for Chartered Secretary at that time for a second string to 'my bow'. So when reality dawned at Dodwell's and relatives of the owners began jumping the queue to fill overseas postings, my early departure became overdue.

Whether by luck or by chance I will never know, but the Daily Telegraph came to my rescue by advertising the Mau Mau emergency raging in Kenya. At last the Crown Agents were looking for me, fancy free and ready to travel. Darkest Africa, with childhood memories of Tarzan and Jane swinging through the trees was the image instilled in my mind from the Saturday morning flicks. But whatever the state of my mind, the advert in the paper had titillated my thoughts, and no matter how wrong my thinking, I applied for the job. In the meantime, I also studied a few books about Kenya to get wise on the subject. Even to this day, No. 4 Mill Bank, on the banks of the Thames is etched in my mind as the place from where my African adventures began. The interviewer was a serving District Commissioner called Bill… someone or other. He was on leave from Kenya and had taken the day off to interview the Telegraph applicants, after which an appointment letter sat on my door-step a few days later. Two points I liked immensely; the princely salary of £864 per annum with 2 increments for my conscripted National Service; it was a life changing offer. Imagine if you can, a few months earlier I had been receiving

28 shillings a week with board and lodging and a free uniform from the Queen. At the end of my 2 year contract in Kenya I was to receive at least 4 days leave per month, depending on the area of my posting. Fort Hall, Muranga, was classified as an unhealthy station and earned 5 days in colonial times, and the Northern Frontier District (NFD) rated 6. How things have changed since then!

At last, a home leave was almost within my grasp like my father and my brother before me. Permanency was offered 9 months into my contract when I was still in Nyeri; I must have been doing something right for a change.

3

Nairobi 1955…

The flaps were down, the engine was barely ticking over and the stillness in the cabin left the passengers straining to hear a movement; at last the wheels touched tarmac. A thin strip of bitumen with a collection of tin huts was the sum total of Eastleigh International Airport Nairobi, some 24 hours from London Heathrow and terminal 3. Any thoughts of a terminal 4 and 5 were still in the clouds, figments of the imagination. En-route, we had landed at Milan, Benghazi, Cairo, Khartoum and Entebbe, where a sniff of the air and a stretch of the legs became routine, and where I suspect some fuel was added.

At the age of 21, this flight for me was a revelation. It was the first time for my feet to leave the ground without the aid of a spring in my steps. On take-off, I was in the clouds with the likes of Orville and Wilbur, enjoying the principle of their flying machine in 1903. Incredible as it may seem, I had remained firmly grounded throughout my service in the Royal Air Force. When posted to Germany in those 'cold-war' years we crossed the English Channel in the bowels of a ship with an empty oil-drum to accommodate the retching. Our transport vessel was the "M.V. Empire Wandsbeck", and it came complete with its 'rust-bucket' qualities to haunt me to this day. In retrospect, we were lucky not to have ended up in Australia with their £10 assisted passages; their immigration policy in the '50s.

The Argonaut, a four-engine piston plane was one of the many owned by the British Overseas Airways Corporation, BOAC, and my fellow passenger next to me in the aisle seat was a British Kenyan farmer called Powys. 'Old man Powys' as he was usually called, separated him from his two youthful sons. The 'Old' man was rightly proud of the massive sheep farm he owned north of Nanyuki, on the grassy slopes of Timau. His hair was white and curly, much like the sheep he herded; but he was at pains to laughingly tell me that his curliness had nothing to do with his choice of farming. During the course of the flight he recounted a short history of his life on the farm and included some interesting tales about his wartime service as a Trooper, foot soldier in the army, before he developed the largest farm in Timau where he now lived. He also mentioned his neighbours, who owned smaller farms than his, much smaller, he emphasised this point, and how they displayed their Officer Ranks from their war service days on their name boards at the end of their drives. Major … Colonel…. Brigadier... no Generals involved. So he had resorted to ridicule them by erecting his own signboard with the designation of the lowest of the low, 'Trooper Powys' to be precise. He enjoyed telling this tale to 'Rookie' Palmer during the flight, and to give him his due, I enjoyed in the listening.

Subsequently, his sons Gilfred and Charles served in Meru District with me and another young boy called Rodney Minns with a family ranch on the Nyeri side of Nanyuki town. Finally, to round up the local 'Kenya cowboys' operating in Meru, there is just one other who springs to mind; Willy Curry, the guy who then had curly blond hair and went on to own and manage the 'Naro Moru River Lodge', which is still in the same beautiful setting today. A prime starting point precisely, to climb Mount Kenya.

The very mention of Rodney Minns conjures up another relic in his time, Larry Wateridge, holder of the Military Medal from the Korean Campaign. Captured by communist forces he told of barefoot marches in sub-zero temperatures; as hard as nails he was, an adventurous spirit by any measure. I subsequently sold him my Ford Consul car used on the Zanzibar safari a year or two into the future, but well before then Larry undertook a rafting expedition from the Tana Falls to the Lamu estuary in cahoots with young Rodney Minns; both as 'Mad as Hatters'. The raft 'drowned' early on in the journey when the anchor snagged between some rocks at one of the falls, to flood the trailing edge by the force of the flow. Undeterred, these fearless adventurers rescued the supplies and acquired a canoe to finish the job; to hell with the giant crocs! Their journey was epic and was one of the firsts from Tana Falls to the Lamu delta by a couple of crazy Whites. Fast forward sixty years and a fearsome grip seizes my arm in the Princess Zara ward at the Aga Khan Hospital; Rodney, like me, was suffering from the ravages of time; strokes, damned strokes, had struck us down. But with God on our side I doubted not, we had the will to survive.

Larry in later years, retired to Mombasa and berthed his yacht at the Club within the harbour reaches. He had dreams of sailing around the world and he almost set out on this venture; he was fully provisioned and the Indian ocean was whispering sweet nothings in his ears. But before he could take up the challenge, his number was called to weigh anchor for a more heavenly place. To this day I remain indebted to Larry for a harbour cruise with Salma my wife in the 1970s. When the three of us vibed as one to sample his dreams, an ethereal wind in our sails.

***

From Eastleigh International Airport to the city centre and Lord Delamere's statue was about two miles, but to get there one had to pass through a heavily guarded majengo area; the Somali enclave. On either side of the road, fortifications told of a city under siege. Houses built of bricks, mud and wattle, were massively defended by barbed wire rolls and ditches with wooden stakes at the bottom. 'Medieval drawbridges' were lowered in daylight hours to permit the free flow of residents, but at night they were raised and reputed to be as 'tight as a drum,' but even such drums as these sprang leaks to prolong the emergency. The struggle for independence was very much in evidence and not an endearing sight. Strange though it may seem in today's world, hardly anyone then walked around in shoes, which shows how life has changed in the present day. But I'll tell you what hasn't changed over time, the generosity of the people with their good humour to make Kenya great. Somehow, and for some strange reason, the ordinary man with no vote in those days remains unchanged, as he uses his new found franchise to elect the greedy, who pocket millions and offer nothing in return.

The Stanbic building, Standard Bank today, bears the same redbrick facade I first set eyes on in the 50s when it was functioning as 'Torrs Hotel', originally built by pioneer Ewart Grogan. 'The Stanley', another premier hotel, was directly opposite Torrs on the other side of Delamere Avenue; it was then only 3 floors high. Its 'Long Bar' was ledgendary, with tall stories to match the hunting of elephant, rhino and anything big. It was usually in full swing and reflected the strength of the beer in hand; regrettably, some years later it was closed. But in the meantime, its main entrance was from the pavement side of the hotel towards the Standard Bank of South Africa and the famous 3 Askari Monument. The historic pictures from the back of the Long Bar were eventually moved to the Norfolk hotel verandah bar, before that too was closed. Fortunately, the easy transfer of historical pictures between two of the finest hotels in Kenya was within the same company, Block Hotels, pioneered and owned by the famous Block family, a Kenya legend in their time. For the record, the pictures have finally settled down in the Norfolk hotel to grace the reception area for your pleasure; may I suggest you seek them out, dwell in the past for a moment and enjoy the history. Compare those scenes with the present day changes and see how they rate?

The Stanley has now increased its stature from three to six floors with a pool-deck on top, but when it was only three high it was difficult to imagine my sharing a beer with Mwai Kibaki up there in 2001; our president in waiting. The third party present was Peter Colemore, a master of Kiswahili broadcasting and a Kikuyu speaker much endeared to Jomo Kenyatta, Kenya's first president. Peter lived in Muthaiga; on occasion I would call in for morning coffee with him and his doctor pathologist friend. Sadly, he passed on a few years later to be eulogized by former attorney general Charles Njonjo in All Saints Cathedral, but it was the Stanley pool-deck in 2001 that witnessed my last meeting with Mwai Kibaki, just before he went on to do greater things; though in the distant past '66 – '69 it was on a more regular basis in the Africa Club, Jivanjee Gardens. On our parting company at the Stanley, Mwai offered to teach me golf and I in return offered to teach him swimming; we were next to the pool at the time, but the twain was never to meet. His presidential aspirations were gaining pace, and understandably so, swimming was not part of his plans.

Equidistant between Torrs and the Stanley buildings, Lord Delamere's statue reclined in an armchair pedestal on a traffic island; the present day crossroads of Kenyatta Avenue and Kimathi Street, regarded as the city centre. Now his likeness is in retirement on the shores of Lake Elmenteita, Soysambu, and the vacant city centre position has been moved ever so slightly towards the new Hilton Hotel, to be occupied by a new national hero, Dedan Kimathi. He stands tall in dashing attire.

***

Nine of us with knees that had yet to be exposed to tropical climes had landed at Eastleigh that morning; the pleasure of our patronage was to be shared between the two biggest hotels in town; that's how we saw it, though perhaps not entirely true. It was the 26th September 1955, and the journey from the airport clearly confirmed that the country had a few difficulties. I reflected then on why I had left Britain, miserable weather, frustrating 'Soap Operas' on TV and the prospect of home-leave after 2 years. Now it was a bit late in the day one way or the other to pause for thought, when adventure in Nyeri lay only hours away.

A bank account had been opened at Barclays, the same yellow building to this day, on the corner of Delamere and Government roads, (Kenyatta and Moi Avenue) using a white British 5 pound note as the initial deposit; a massive amount of money in those days. That piece of white paper was left behind by the thief who thought it worthless, when selecting the pound and ten shilling notes from my wallet as I relaxed in the bath at the end of the corridor. En-suite was the dream of the rich and only an idiot would have left a wallet lying around in a strange country; it was my own fault entirely. However, my loss was mellowed when I heard about the waiter's exploits as my colleagues' munched a hearty breakfast in the Thorn Tree Restaurant at the Stanley. The gap between the backrest and the seat had proved irresistible to the 'waiting' staff when they saw the bums and back pockets on offer; that was the theory behind their loses, but no one knew for sure. We packed our bags, loaded the Land Rovers and pushed on to Ahmed Bros, the camping equipment merchant doing a roaring trade on the back of the Emergency. From there we took possession of a camp bed, a canvas bath, and a film director's camp chair, using our government allowances for house-building in the reserve. At last we were fully equipped to bear the ravages of Africa; Wilbur Smith the author, had yet to know of our existence, as we had yet to know of his.

Kenya was blessed with 131 miles of tarmac outside the townships. 100 to Nakuru, 26 to Thika, and a 5-mile patch at McKinnon Road on the way to Mombasa; strategically placed to deceive the traveller into thinking they'd arrived at the coast. We were now on the 26 miles of tarmac in the direction of Thika, using the District Commissioner's Land

Rover to announce to the world we're on Safari, adventure is our purpose. As we passed through Thika some idiot asked if the pineapples were small palms trees, and other members of our party were keeping a sharp eye out for the likes of Tarzan and Jane swinging through the trees. Such ignorance embraced an expectant air, as we picked up speed on the murram road to cross the new Sagana Bridge. Half an hour later we were chugging-up 'Pole Pole Hill', pronounced like roly poly, which brought us to the rail track entering Karatina with 20 miles of road to Nyeri town; our journey was almost over.

4

The layout of Nyeri town in the 1950s was nothing remarkable, a large village well fits the picture. It was the capital of Central Province, and one of the places where the emergency is believed to have started. Development had yet to take hold of the open fields within the township, presently used for cattle grazing. The built up area stretched from the Government Hospital as you arrive from Karatina via Ruringu Stadium, to the Garden Hospital in the north just off the Ihururu road, where a barrier separates the town from fantastic trout fishing in the Sagana river valley. To the West, senior staff houses were in the vicinity of the Green Hills Hotel of today; they overlooked the golf course from West to East with the famous cemetery in the distance on the other side of town. The Ministry of Works was halfway down the hill on the Kiganjo road, with the Tree Tops turnoff to the left on the other side of the ravine; the same area where the girls school functioned and the new prison was under construction. The roads within the township were only partly tarmac and did not extend beyond Winters Garage in the direction of the Government General Hospital, nor beyond the Ihururu division barrier. Finally, the old fortified Police Armoury, before the town exit towards Kiganjo also needed some serious road construction.

The Outspan Hotel is beautifully laid out for everyone's enjoyment and it remains the same to this very day. Its place in history is assured by Lord Baden Powell the founder of the Boy Scouts movement, who lived there as a long-time guest from 1938 to 1941. His room of many years is preserved in his memory and worthy of a visit, after which, take a healthy walk down the No.1. fairway to his final resting place in the Nyeri cemetery, facing Mount Kenya.

My life of luxury over the next twelve months was a room at the Outspan Hotel; the main entrance remains unchanged to this day but the inside bars are now redesigned and rearranged. So let's revert to '55 and the old lounge to the left as you pass through the main entrance, which stretches to the front lawns and offers majestic views of the mountain and the Aberdares, tinged by the setting sun on occasion; and if you get really lucky, the white snow turns to pink before your very eyes as one more day hits the dust. Halfway down this same passageway is the reception desk and the dining room entrance with a wood-panelled minstrels' gallery under which diners must pass. The waiters were always pristinely dressed in white khanzu, red cummerbund and red fez hats; all of which were replaced at Independence with trousers and tunics to look less servile, so the story goes. Another change of dress was from the shorts worn by the 'Wazungu', Europeans, to long trousers favoured by the 'Wananchi', Africans; the reason given was, school boys wear shorts and officials didn't look so official if they wore the same... Hence, any display of knobbly colonial knees was out of fashion for the *new boys* on the block!

If there are three recently acquired friends having dinner on a first evening out of Nairobi, or anywhere else for that matter, it surely follows that one of the three has been out of England before. So he wishes to dispense some of the wisdom picked up on his travels to the other 'peasants', captive to hear his tale.

hin"kI It should warn you two before it happens," the 'old hand' from Saudi Arabia dropped his remarks from out of the blue.

"About what?" the man from Huddersfield shovelled another piece of fish into his mouth and chewed as he waited for an answer.

"About the hazards… before you get into your bed tonight." ex-Saudi Arabia was serious, dead serious, and kept a sullen face to match the gravity of his words; he was also enjoying his moment to impress his captive audience.

"Okay, I'll buy it. What's wrong with the beds?" my curiosity wanted to know.

"Well; we're in the tropics and in the tropics…" he hesitated, to keep us hanging…

"What's so important in the tropics?" 'Huddersfield' fell into the trap; his mouthful of fish was still a mouthful of fish, and it hadn't yet to hit the 'spot'.

"Well… when you go to bed tonight make sure you turn back your sheets completely. Check for snakes!" he suitably hissed his warning to deliver his dubious message.

"Never heard of such rubbish," I said. But before I went to bed that night I turned back my sheets and checked them out; wouldn't you do the same?

Turn to the left as you pass through the main entrance and the hotel lounge bears witness to numerous unusual happenings, but being in Nyeri I was told they weren't that unusual at all.

So I'll let you judge for yourself about one such happening that I believed to be more comical than most, and it had nothing to do with the noisy bedsprings in number 14 occupied by a certain young lady; best left untold. It was all about a visiting dog around tea time, who enjoyed the hotel food. He was of Labrador breed and his coat was black, so it was not surprising when one of the guests declared his name to be 'Blackie'. And you could set a watch by Blackie's appearance in the lounge at 4 pm. He was always hungry and his drooling attitude helped to solicit the occasional cake or passing sandwich before it reached your mouth; none of us believed we were teaching the dog bad habits by feeding him at mealtimes, which was exactly what we were doing. And little did we realise that, the staff in the flowing khanzu and red fez hats were obliged to keep an eye-out for unusual activities during the old colonial ritual of tea-drinking, cucumber sandwiches and cream cakes. Such as feeding visitors free of charge, the dog in this case was frowned upon, not to go unnoticed. This became apparent when the staff informed Sherbrook Walker the hotel owner, about Blackie's participation in our tea-drinking ceremonies at 4 pm sharp. Apparently, Blackie was not the Hotel dog we had supposed him to be, and his exact origin or residence wasn't known. A fact borne out by a message attached to his collar one afternoon… "This dog visits the hotel on a regular basis to eat food offered to him by guests, and if he continues with these visits you will be charged for the food he eats." Signed, Sherbrook Walker. He mysteriously disappeared after that warning, the dog, not Walker, and life carried on without our furry friend. A nice interlude had come to an end.

Many a yarn came home to roost before this Sherry Bar incident I'm about to recall. Had we turned to the left on passing through the hotel lobby, I would have been obliged to mention the Land Rover driven down the hallway steps to check-in a guest at midnight, but for the present we'll bear to the right and concentrate on the original tale I had in mind.

The Sherry Bar was a 'watering-hole' of considerable note and a cosy place to be of an evening. The usual crowd would normally gather towards sundown, an hour before the dinner gong summoned the hungry. In this modern age when standards are slipping, it's amazing to note that the same gong with a different beat was also struck half an hour earlier for guests to start dressing for dinner; a custom alive and kicking back then. But the modern day guests now ask 'what's that,' if it sounds at all, then they expect to see some tribal dancing. Eating dinner dressed in shorts and string-vests with unwashed hairy armpits was frowned upon in the past, as was the drinking of beer from a bottle when a perfectly good glass was provided. The birth of the 'trough' and manners to match had yet to dawn; but watch out for these modern day freaks with bums hanging out of their jeans, they're now on the march to break the rules of civilised living.

Summoned by the second gong, residents would depart for the dining room. It was also the signal for those not staying at the hotel to get stuck-in and continue drinking before the others returned to round off the evening. To reach this cosy drinking den one would pass under the hotel portal and bear right past the room with the hole in the wall for the cinema projector. A cinematographic experience of a Saturday night was a regular feature, and the old fashioned word cinematographic best describes these shows that were given free by the government information department. They usually featured Charlie Chaplin, Laurel and Hardy, a few of the old greats with harmless humour. Since then however, the hotel has moved on and the hole in the projection room wall is now the only memento of the past; if indeed it's still there?

Continue further down this corridor and we'll arrive at the place where I was originally headed; the sherry bar beyond the conference room-cum-cinema auditorium. Today this sherry bar area is the Tree-Tops Lodge reception centre, and if history from the fifties could tell tales about that room there would be many; so let me mention just one event to spark your interest as the cobwebs from a less ancient past listen in. There was always a pleasant mix in the sherry bar and I'm not talking about the drinks, I'm talking about the people. The young Administrative Assistants, of which I was one, were usually trying to outdo the military officers with inflated tales about their exploits in the Aberdares. And as the evenings wore-on they became more and more outrageous; the last man left standing then declared himself the winner. After which he staggered towards his vehicle, to speed off into the night.

The administrators of the time usually wore baggy khaki shorts, Bata safari boots at 28 bob a pair, and a military pattern short sleeved jacket would be a design of your preference. A gun belt that holstered a pistol, was also of your choice. Uniformity was just not there, and to justify the sloppy dress code 'everyone was fighting a war', so to speak. Where and how was not quite clear, but that was the excuse put forward to cover the odd shapes and sizes. The rule of thumb for side-arms was, the rougher the Kenyan cowboy the bigger the gun, and anyone who had been in the army usually toted a .45 revolver that kicked like a mule. It would surely take a man down if the bullet only grazed his thumb; a powerful tool it certainly was.

On occasion and without too much encouragement, the

playing cards fixed on the bar ceiling were inclined to dance in time to the number of Tusker beers consumed at Shs.1.40 a bottle. To the British army, the 'dancing card' was usually a recipe for hot discussion as the crowd increased and the evening wore on. The sherry bar was one of the army officer's favourite 'watering holes', although the prices were twice those in the officers' mess, where a bottle of whisky crossed the counter at 15 shillings. On this one particular evening, conversation was running fast and no-one knew to where it would lead. As a comparative new-comer, I was sitting in a dark corner with Colin Hamilton the information guy and KBC broadcaster of the future, who exhibited the occasional film through the hole in the wall in the next-door room. The third man in our company was a D.O. Kikuyu Guard, like we were all gazetted to be. He was rather unusual in that he was learning to drive with the help of a Hillman Minx coupe, the coolest model of the day.

Trouble was brewing and loud voices filled the room; it was then that the challenge rang out to settle the argument once and for all. An obnoxious army major declared himself to be a magnificent shot and to prove his point, he would shoot a hole in one of the red Hearts stuck on the bar ceiling. The ceiling décor was a mix of playing cards, Hearts, Spades, Diamonds, Clubs, and to shoot a hole in one of the Hearts was more convincing to him than any of the other symbols. As he looked for the card on the ceiling, he demanded to know from the DO at his side if he even knew where the trigger was on his own pistol. To follow up his question he shouted "amateurs, bloody amateurs, that's what you are!" This loud declaration was still ringing in everyone's ears as he struggled to draw his .45 out of its holster, but in the course of its drawing the gun went off and a second ringing was heard in everyone's ears. The explosion of a .45 pistol in that confined space was so deafening that all argument ceased, and for the first time that evening the room was deathly silent. It was then noticed that the barman was missing when the drinks ran out. True enough, the barman was indeed missing and he had to be found, since a missing barman during a busy period was a serious matter, almost beyond belief. It then transpired he wasn't missing at all, he was merely 'resting' on the floor inside the bar clutching his wounded leg. Some wit declared 'man down' NYPD style, and another intoxicated idiot asked why the barman had changed his customary serving position from being there, to being nowhere in sight?

Years later, I heard the happy ending to this story when in conversation with Jane Kiano, my long time friend from Tumu Tumu Mission, the Panafric Hotel, and a member of the Nguyo dynasty; also wife to Julius, minister of commerce in Kenyatta's first cabinet. She declared the man behind the bar to have been her uncle and added that, he was only grazed and returned to work a few weeks later with no hard feelings. On reflection, I have to admit that this type of accident was not an isolated incident; it was inclined to happen rather frequently during the emergency and no one was ever held to account. Impunity was the name of the game away back then, and in the present day it's become as 'bold as brass'.

This was a sign of the times in Nyeri, but as my life progressed improvement was in the air, or so it seemed to me as I worked on the fringe of my chosen projects over the next twelve months. Frankly speaking, chasing the Mau Mau in the Aberdares was for 'the birds'; they were few and far between and hard to find in '56, or perhaps they'd become more invisible as they perfected their forest skills. Nevertheless, out of curiosity rather than duty, I ventured into the bamboo thickets to undertake the impossible task of flushing something out. By then, the Mau Mau was using well worn animal tracks that tunnelled through bamboo walls into the forest heartland. So during the chase, if you could describe it as such, you were usually bent double to pass through the smallest of thickets; and serious chasers wouldn't wash for weeks to hide their soapy smells from veteran forest fighters. In retrospect, I believe such habits saved on 'LUX', (no advertising intended) and possibly, tongue in cheek, reduced climate change, but only the 'experts' who craft fat careers on the backs of disasters and luxury meetings would know about that. Fast forward to 2018, and I'm exercising of an early morning in the company of freshly showered young ladies on their way to work. The power of their soapy scent rekindles memories of the Aberdares when once I was young; their present day youth leaves me gasping!

Many of the rooms at the Outspan Hotel were of wooden construction; my Banda (circular hut) was no exception. Full board and lodging at Shs.750 per month was the tariff, Shs.250 of which was subsidized by the government. Luxury provided at a reasonable cost sums up entirely my living high in 1956. There were no en-suites at this price, so I would take a hike to the lavatory on a cold stone path after a night in the bar; I was young enough to take the shock. Banda occupiers also had the option to use the good old colonial standby of 'watering the flowers' in the garden after dinner; this facility was behind my room on a patch where the plants appeared vicious, I was merely striking back. And in these modern times of gender equality, circumstances permitting, I wouldn't be surprised to hear of the ladies playing similar tricks.

An additional one million pounds a month was allocated for emergency activities in addition to normal recurrent expenditure; from these extra funds all sorts of goodies flowed. One such item that came my way was an Austin Champ, far advanced in its time. After taking delivery of this vehicle I was bound to get a driving licence to regularise my activities, though there was little chance of being stopped to show my credentials; an emergency was in progress to excuse anomalies. But the law is the law, so I booked my test with the local Asian police inspector, who had the reputation of passing all the beautiful young Asian ladies, which put me at a disadvantage. The message then hit home when he failed me twice; a cheeky devil he surely was! So I switched to a European inspector who might be on my side and passed with flying colours; may God bless his finer judgment.

The driving license booklet I now use was issued in Nyeri on 8th November 1955. Of robust materials it presently serves me well, while its antique status grows by the day.

5

Looking back over the years, it is clear to me that I failed to achieve my yearning for active service whatever my endeavours. The guardian angel sitting on my shoulder was always looking after my safety, and for that consideration I suppose, I should be eternally grateful. Imagine this; I joined the Royal Air Force at the time of the Korean War and applied for active service in the Far East; that's where the fighting was and that's where my talents were needed; my opinion entirely. So, as usual, my request was ignored and I was drafted to West Germany on active service during the Cold War; a frozen war with frozen action describes it well. Imagine, the powers that be wouldn't even issue live ammunition for guard duty, lest one of us irresponsible fellows triggered World War 3. That was the status quo when I was forced to wear the Queen's uniform to defend the nation in 1952. It was either conscripted national service or jail, and I preferred the former. Western Europe was the posturing place where nothing ever happened, with or without ammunition. As a result, our guard duties embraced a relaxing Woodbine cigarette in the shadows of a shed, thereby avoiding the blame for sparking a WW3. I don't deny the Russians were causing disturbances at the time, but the only claim I have to any action in that particular sphere was an overnight stay in an Austrian jail caused by the Russians, and not of my doing. It was my bad luck to be en-route to Vienna by train the very day Stalin chose to die. True, we were released the following morning without explanation, but by then we had been staring at Stalin's portrait draped in black ribbons for 24 hours. Displayed to emphasise the fact that, the murdering bugger had at last kicked the bucket and joined the millions he'd denied the right to live. We then re-boarded the train at Melk to reach Vienna intact.

Nyeri District was another one of my attempts to be where the action was, but on arrival the British army was busy pulling out having done their duty, whatever that was? In the mean time their tents were pitched on the fields between Winters Garage, and the Nyeri General Hospital, the place where Field Marshall Dedan Kimathi was eventually admitted with a wounded leg. At the time, local gossip told of Kimathi's previous employment in the shop of Jack Wright the butcher, before he was discovered in history to be a person of intellect. But whatever his persuasion, his freedom struggle gained weight with his activities in the Aberdares. The butcher was not the only European shopkeeper in Nyeri town at this time. Norman Pring the chemist also springs to mind, with his corner shop opposite Osman Allu's. But as far as shops were concerned, you mention it and Allu's had been selling the same since the 1920s; BP and Caltex petrol from their road-side pumps were the first in town; Asian ingenuity at its best. Mister Hamilton was another shopkeeper-cum-farmer on the Kiganjo road, who could never resist a mean shilling. I had on occasion seen the sale of a single cigarette to squeeze that extra cent. Winters

Garage, the Outspan Hotel of Sherbrook Walker and the White Rhino Hotel also had their European connections.

Outside the township, the farming community were some of the most vibrant profit producers in the country. Many farms bordered the main road from Nyeri to the Kiganjo Police Training School and beyond; they produced rich rewards for the roasting of coffee berries at £600 per ton. During my time at the Outspan, I got to know the Evan's farm just 4 miles up the road, where I had an open invitation to use their tennis court. Mrs Evans was never around, but her farm manager who became my friend, was running the show. Urs van Dryl was a Dutchman, his wife who was called Pat was English, and they had a beautiful little girl between them. As custom had it, such staff was recruited directly from Europe before independence and generous inducements were offered. For example, Urs was looking forward to an annual coffee bonus of £800 in addition to his salary, which demonstrated the wealth generated by the industry in '56; it was the price of a Mercedes saloon if you had the inclination.

Paddy Aiken, a member of the administration in Nyeri, had a surplus in his emergency building vote at the end of the financial year, 30th June 1956, and the Provincial Commissioner had a brilliant idea to mop up the savings. They would be used to erect an obelisk in the centre of Nyeri town to honour the Loyalists, who had sacrificed their lives in fighting the Mau Mau menace. On completion, the masterpiece was unveiled by the P.C. Frank Lloyd, and all those present praised Paddy's architectural skills for a job well done. The brass plaque embedded in the stone explained the shadows cast in the centre of town, there to pay tribute to the fallen loyalists. However, several years later the monolith became an embarrassment to the new elite who had sided with the Colonial Government, not to mention those who had emerged from the bamboo thickets to claim their dreams; to remain their dreams forever. To a few genuine fighters the metal plaque was rightly offensive, and the loyalists didn't want to be reminded of their chosen side before and after independence; so one night the label disappeared to join the trappings of abandoned history hidden by hate. For the record, it was inscribed, 'In honour of those loyalists who lost their lives in the course of the emergency' etcetera, etcetera. Right now, this symbolic monolith in the centre of Nyeri Town is interpreted to suit the imaginations of young historians, but the original plaque if ever found deserves a place in the national archives, provided it hasn't been shipped off to China to help with the current scrap metal drive. Bronze fetches high prices so I am told, and the engraving by Wali Mohammed in Nairobi could only be 'Chinese' to the Chinese.

Unfortunately, Michela Wrong got it wrong in her book, "It's Our Turn to Eat". She missed the unveiling and had to rely on gossip, and gossip in Kenya is gossip in Kenya; it has been known to stretch the mind on many occasions. The loss of life during the emergency was tragic, and over the 5-year period it was estimated to be in the thousands, but an accurate figure for this shame is just not there. When I last saw the monument its empty meaning was very empty, but something has to appear in the next few years to make the county voters happy, and of course, the tenderpreneurs. They could even add some recent follies to match this folly, such as a small Bungoma wheelbarrow or perhaps a local hospital bed worth millions, to warn against corrupt adventures. Fortunately, the plinth is too small to build on or to be grabbed, but watch this space and see what happens.

Wretched fellows were paraded before the Magistrates court next to the Provincial Offices on a regular basis; heavy rusty leg-irons and manacles were worn on these occasions. Chains also linked the legs and hands so they couldn't take-off. They had been caught in the forest, and from their sallow faces they always looked hungry, and once again they were being paraded without any efforts from me. It was then that I decided to turn my attention to other things; improving the lot of the law-abiding locals by using the emergency regulations to 'lean' on the Chiefs, who would in turn 'lean' on the villagers to produce 20/- a hut. Subsequently, I used this collection to purchase Blake's Hydram water pumps from Alibhai Shariff in Nairobi; circular brick-built tanks from fast flowing streams had to be filled. The water was then filtered through sand before reaching a fancy tap to serve little old ladies. Imagine if you can, my pleasure at seeing such people filling jerry-cans from a tap for the first time in their lives; I enjoyed my selfish reward. My biggest enterprise was pipedwater into Gatitu village administered by Chief William, a likable rotund character in charge of the area before Wambugu Farm Institute came into being.

    I was virtually my own boss in Nyeri and worked from the Health Office, with overall guidance from Health Inspectors Ernest Jones and Bernard Shaw. My transport and part finances came via their offices to fulfil a public health duty, a role I enjoyed immensely. Today, I'm led to believe that many of the water tanks I built are still in situ, but I haven't been back to check the facts and most probably, I never will. Most of the civil service in those times imagined a Mau Mau to be hiding behind every tree, and I as a naïve individual believed them to be in the forest, or perhaps they were drinking tea to wash down the vitamins pills handed out in detention camps by the crazy British. The trappings of the emergency activity continued as though no-one wanted it to end, and like Bin Laden, when the elusive Dedan Kimathi was caught in 1956, things had already collapsed and a new scene entirely was on the horizon. However, for some self-serving logical reasons, with which I agreed, the colonial government was prolonging the emergency to enjoy a couple of extra years on their pensions. And as for the settlers, they were quite content to live in peace as they waited for the buy-out programme courtesy of the U.K. Budget.

6

In 1956 my timing would have placed me in early Spring had I been living in England, but by now I was well settled at the Outspan Hotel in Nyeri, a short distance from the DC's office where the Union flag was alive and kicking, despite many wishes of the local players to bury it early! In the final analysis many years hence, Independence was either graciously granted or grabbed, it was a case of which side you fought on and how you looked best; that's human nature I guess?

I don't like to admit it and I may well be wrong as I have been a few times before, but when I arrived in Kenya it seemed as though the emergency was almost over and posed little threat to civil society. So I would usually walk to work in Nyeri, unarmed and defenceless, using the golf-course fairway that stretched as far as the Admin Offices where the 'big wigs' managed the province. Frank Lloyd, a small dapper man with super intelligent eyes, was the Provincial Commissioner. He didn't have the title of 'Excellency', though he flew a small Union Jack on his vehicle exhibiting a touch of colonial pomp; now much in demand by the new elite in present day Kenya. Rumour has it that bells, whistles and 'chase cars' are still in their formative stages today, but rumours, as I've said before, are only rumours Kenya style. For a short a period, Doctor Ken Craig the Provincial Medical Officer, was my boss and one of the nicest personalities in town. Jim Pedraza, a giant of a man who never got flustered, filled the post of District Commissioner. In my eyes, these two guys were running the show on the ground and were the cream of governance in '55. And on the other side of the coin in direct contrast to their august positions was I, the size of a fresh tick on a donkey, about to begin my learning curve.

What a wonderful way to start the day by dwelling on my future and good-fortune, to have left the London smog behind for others to cough and splutter. Those were my regular thoughts when I chose to walk and breathe mountain air rather than drive. I would pick up my wheels at lunchtime, no sandwiches and flask of tea for me in the office when I remained in town, a full lunch always hit the spot. I was young and slender at the time, but should I choose to take a lunch box and soft drink from the hotel for a picnic in the country side, it always seemed to end in disaster.

There was no-one around at first, as I chose an ideal spot beside a babbling brook; the noise of cascading water flowing over rounded pebbles was magic to behold. The rich green grass cropped by the sheep and goats was like a finely mown lawn, and the desertion of the spot was usually blessed by the shade of an indigenous tree. I would then sit on the grass in the shade and begin to munch my sandwiches to the relaxing sound of the flowing water in the background; then all of a sudden things would change in a flash like they always did; whether a carefully chosen site or not, made absolutely no difference. The goats, the sheep, the cattle, the dogs and anything else that could possibly get to my picturesque setting was suddenly there! I was occupied, and their smell had also come along with a bunch of flies they couldn't leave behind. This was just the animal contingent, before the hungry watoto (kids) from the village on the other side of the hill pitched-up with pleading eyes to watch my every bite; of a hitherto juicy sandwich. By then my lunch had lost its taste to a silent staring, so intense that I had to abandon my eating and what was left to those who needed it most. News travels fast in the reserve whatever its merits, and I was the attraction for miles around that day. As usual, I always said 'never again', but the temptation was always too strong, so more often than not I ended up with a whole tribe in the bush due to my stubborn nature.

I was expected to do my own driving and maintenance tasks on the Austin Champ vehicle that displayed the standard OHMS number, prior to GK post-independence. There was also a brief period of RGA plates, Regional Government Agent, when the provinces were changed to regions before Majimboism crashed. The Austin Champ was a wonderful vehicle; all steel construction and somewhat unusual with 5 forward gears and 5 in reverse; full torsion-bar suspension and no conventional springs was also part of the package. The single fuel tank held 16 gallons plus, and the attendant was usually looking for leaks when the 10-gallon mark was passed at the pump. Its canvas roof tamed the weather, and the open sides offered cavalier rides as standard.

Much like the many veterans of World War II who thought it was a wonderful war and hoped it would go on forever, I also found myself getting ready for an emergency, when I knew it was on the wane. But, being an adventurous spirit, I embarked on a spending spree for some fancy items I really didn't need. I'd never owned nor fired one before, but it was offered for sale by a man going back to the UK; a 9 mm Luger pistol for the princely sum of Shs. 100 or £5, such was the exchange rate in those days. And fortunately for my pocket it used the same stengun ammunition supplied by the government, to feed a weapon that usually jammed when most needed.

The youngest Assistant Superintendent of Police in the country was Bill Blackwell, who was promoted by his seniors in advance of his years when they heard of his Mau Mau exploits, subsequently told to me. It was all about a sten-gun jamming with him on the end of such a misfortune. At the time he was almost overrun by an attacking force in a bamboo clearing in the Aberdares; his police support had left him to fend for himself and a defiant gesture was needed. He drew his .45 pistol in a last ditch stand; 'Colonel Custer fighting off Indians springs to mind', and with only two shots remaining his blood curdling noises made the enemy take-off, much like his police escort had, in the opposite direction. This epic event was relayed to me by Bill in raconteur fashion during an evening work-out; we were pressing 'iron' in his old wooden house in Nyeri at the time.

So my luger purchase had merit and used sten-gun ammunition; not that I was about to wage war, but the saving of a few shillings here and there was to my advantage. A transfer form was completed from seller to buyer and rubber stamped by the Police, a few formalities and certainly no 'good conduct certificate' as of today was needed. On the other hand you were severely warned to keep your weapon under lock and key, so I rarely carried the 'thing' around; it became my 'ball and chain'. My policy was to let the askaris do the guarding; well, they were the professionals.

The next item on my shopping list was some type of uniform, the choice of which was left up to the individual. No flamboyant badges were used. And be assured, should one fall short of expectations snide remarks would soon be heard from so called 'friends'. I also commissioned the local shoemaker to craft a pair of calf-high leather boots to compliment my long woollen socks, worn just below the knees. By then, some well intentioned friends said I looked a bit of a mess, but I couldn't see it at the time. The legs of my khaki shorts were also worthy of note; 20 inches wide and designed to keep ones 'tackle' cool. Where the shorts were concerned such uniqueness of design had evolved over the years to call them 'settler fashions'. However, the bush jacket, 'the icing on the cake', had four patch-pockets similar to Kimathi's statue in sight of the Hilton Hotel today. It also boasted of brass buttons with the Kenya lion rampant, freshly purloined from the admin. stores. (See photo Baringo District with escort). Decades into the future, I sigh as I reminisce about a full head of hair that precluded the wearing of any type of head-gear. On the whole, the administration service was reasonably informal in the 50s and chugged along without too much hot air. I had just spent 2 years of my life doing National Service for Queen and country in uniform on parade, so I for one was prepared to operate in low key. Further regimentation wasn't about to creep up on me in any shape or form, which generously left the Queen's birthday parades for the enjoyment of others. But when my absence might be noticed, I would wear a suit and stand in the crowd, as I was obliged to do.

Whilst on the subject of uniform, regimentation dwells in my mind as I recall a weak moment when I was ambushed by Paddy Aiken to join the Kenya Regiment, a friend and an Irishman to boot, who boasted of having shaken the hand of King George V1 some time in his past. I was impressed by his claim to have been touched by royalty, but not by his intention to join the Regiment. Apparently, his Irishness had denied him national service, and for some reason at this late date the regiment was recruiting as though the emergency had years to go. Paddy declared the uniform to come for free, and I in turn declared, nothing comes for free and he counts me out. Whether he joined or not I cannot recall, but while I'm on the subject of Paddy, dear chap that he was, let me digress about some of the things that occupied him in Nyeri. As I have previously stated, he left his mark in the form of an obelisk, which I was able to compare with my own building activities and question the more courageous. I grudgingly awarded Paddy the prize.

He would leave an epitaph to his name with a modern day Whitehall Cenotaph in Nyeri town, and I had only been building wards at the General Hospital 'supervised' by Dedan Kimathi. I still regret to this day not questioning Kimathi as to how he was caught; no fuss surrounded him at the time and he wasn't about to go anywhere with a leg plaster and his hands in cuffs. The fellow was laid back on white pillows with his wounded leg slightly elevated out of harm's way, and he seemed to be enjoying the afternoon sun as he watched my progress without emotion. Those are the facts and no hearsay is involved. I can also confirm his famous picture on the front of the East African Standard broad sheet edition was an exact likeness, and I'm the first to admit that I only said 'hujambo' to him because I didn't know he spoke English. My Swahili was still rather limited by the short time I'd spent in the country. Missing this golden opportunity to hear his story, I shall regret for the rest of my life. Sunday, 21st October '56 was the precise date of his capture, and when I saw him he was still wearing the same dreadlocks tied up on top of his head, matched by the shagginess of an unkempt beard. In my estimation, his most striking feature that 'stood out a mile', was a searching glint in his jet-black eyes from years in the forest. He'd been shot in the thigh as he ran beside a red murram road synonymous of Othaya, North Tetu. In the sights of a vigilant loyalist enforcing the law he didn't stand a chance. The maroon jersey, leather shoulder pads and pillbox hat never knew the magnitude of his historic deed at the time, and perhaps it remains obscure to this day, but I have no doubt there will be a claim to fame or shame in the future, and I sympathise with whoever? In the passage of time imaginations run wild and doubtful versions about what actually happened are bound to surface; but rest assured, hearsay Kenya style will fill in all the blanks. (Actual date of capture was recorded by Ian Henderson's, 'Hunt for Kimathi')

'Home made guns' can be viewed in the Nairobi National Museum, and houses in England have been known to decorate their walls with such mementos hanging over their fireplaces. The rifle stocks were usually made of roughly hewn wood, smallbore water pipes were used for barrels and door-bolt firing-pins were energised by rubber car inner tubing. On occasion, these weapons had cleverly devised finger triggers, but more often than not the bolt to fire the cartridge was released by hand and could be dangerous. An ingenious 'U' shaped piece of metal was sometimes used to fire different sizes of ammunition in the same weapon; the idea was brilliant, but the machining was crude and dangerous to use. When a person was captured in possession of such a weapon the government would run a test to prove it lethal or otherwise; the purpose was to charge the fellow in possession with whatever the test concluded. A capital offence could have been committed when the carrier was found in possession of a lethal weapon; the law was a stickler and the charge had to be just right, whatever the rumour doing the rounds. During these tests the gun was mounted in a .303 tripod rest with a long piece of string attached to the bolt-action. It was thought wise to take cover behind a wall or the side of a house before pulling the string, and when such common sense prevailed, no accidents that I knew of occurred. If the weapon fired and the bullet supplied by the government rolled out of the tube it was deemed quite lethal, but if the bullet didn't get to the end of the tube it was declared quite harmless. Sometimes they fired properly and sometimes they didn't; so it was usually 'the luck of the draw' as to who was charged, 'found-in-possession'.

For official events the Provincial Commissioners and DCs continued to wear 'whites' complete with ceremonial sword, Bombay Bowler or pith helmet, a throwback from Imperial India. The Queen's birthday parade was one of these more painful events I was bound to attend, as one of the crowd I would wear my dark suit that could easily double for funerals and evening events. A genuine multi-task bit of cloth it definitely was, some wit actually thought I'd slept in it on one occasion when it was badly creased; but to double for pyjamas, it could not. The dressing up in 'whites' was running out of time, so even the keenest of new DO's was shamelessly saving the coins and using that 'little dark suit' symbolic of 'that little black dress' women wear for everything these days, including cocktails and *me-too* functions.

About this time of pomp and confusion, the peace lovers in the country required a reduction in 'maundu mau', those things, to feel the emergency was over. This left the settlers as anxious as the government loyalists, each with their own inner fears and agendas. On one hand there was a doubtful future for the settlers, and on the other the loyalists were aching for the power they'd earned when they sided with the colonial government to end the violence. The national movement, the loudest voice in the country, knew exactly what was about to happen. Independence was on the brink and the emergency funding to central province was on the way out, with only a few years left to run. A small portion of this additional money from the British government was now being used to subsidise village water projects and extra hospital wards. On the plus side and for the benefit of my ego, the hospital wards remain intact as an epitaph to my struggles; they also mark the spot of many meetings with Dedan Kimathi.

The Nyeri town commercial centre revolved around the good business sense of Osman Allu, the largest family grocer on the corner; two rows of shops extended on either side to the West and the South. Osman Allu's could be likened to the leader of a flock of geese in full flight with the left wing represented by Nyeri Provision Store towards the White Rhino Hotel, and on the right wing was the Nyeri Camera Shop on the high street, where I purchased my Eumig cine to capture the 1956 Coronation Safari Rally. The safari checkpoint was at Winters Garage the Land Rover agent, and in case you're wondering about the outcome of the safari let me put your mind at rest; the magnificent DKW auto union of Eric Cecil collected the laurels that year.

Incidentally, all camera equipment was duty free in Kenya at this time; I suspect it was for the benefit of the British army at Gil Gil, but who knows? The mention of Gil Gil encourages me to reminisce with a quick trip to Nairobi from Nakuru, using the 100 miles of tarmac built by the Italian prisoners of war in the 1940s. If you ever find yourself on this route, do stop at the church that nestles in the hairpin bend before you climb the escarpment; say a prayer for your safety on the road where God is great and the drivers are lousy!

Let's now switch back to Nyeri Provision's and Osman Allu's the Settlers banker's, and the only professional bank in town that was adjacent to the Law Courts next door to the DC's complex. The Standard Bank of South Africa stood aloof from the traders and was very much on its own; it was not in the grocery business and didn't serve settlers with provisions, nor did it offer any form of credit with a supply of food up front before the harvest. The Standard Bank of South Africa was in business under this same name for decades before its 'chickens came home to roost' in '59. The words 'South Africa' then disappeared from their buildings overnight with no fanfare or announcement, new cheque books were only issued when the old ran out. Historically, Osman Allu was the first shop in Nyeri village; it was established around 1894 by a man called Osman who stepped ashore from a Bombay steamer with all the natural skills of a shop keeper. Nyeri Provision Store was always trying to catch up, but both in their time had acted as the white settler's bankers for as long as anyone could remember. Their over-the-counter prices were high, but in return they carried debts on the strength of a signature until the crops came in. Coffee prices were also high in the late 50s, and be assured, 'black-gold' was first used to describe this bonanza long before oil took the title.

7

My time for a sojourn in Meru arrived towards the end of the last quarter in 1956. Apparently, the powers that be required my accounting expertise on the other side of the mountain. A District Revenue Office was about to be established for the very first time. Someone, somewhere, had been studying my CV and had noticed a knowledge of accounts was within my grasp. Meru, 80 miles to the northeast of Nyeri, was just around the mountain and hitherto only a speck on the map. It was now about to become a fully fledged adventure for me, a reality, in fact. It was also to be a new experience for Meru to get a brand new revenue chap in a brand new job; so the district and I were in this thing together. On arrival, I had to make 'waves' for a space to be cleared on the back verandah of the DC's office; old box files were shoved aside to make room for my tiny chair, and God at that time only knew where the table would fit. Challenged at first I surely was, but I was there to 'spread my wings' with no second thoughts on the matter.

Meru was moving up in the world. The administrative staff that checked the accounting skills of the district cashier were about to retire; their tinkering with the accounts was now to be part of my job; not to tinker, but to check properly. And I must confess when I first looked into the district cash office a shakeup was long overdue. I thought back to my accounting activities in London and queried their effectiveness in the African bush…2 plus 2 would always be 4, and that's as far as it got!

The transfer procedure was usually a gentlemanly exercise. It could take as much as a couple of weeks to wind up your affairs before shaking the hand of the DC Meru, who would have arranged your *place in the sun* on arrival. In my case it was to be 'The Pig and Whistle Hotel', owned and managed by a swarthy middle aged man called Stringer. Throughout my government service, bachelors were usually treated as second-class citizens compared to the married man, but I must confess that I had enjoyed my stay at the Outspan Hotel without the hassle of managing a household, which could never have been the luck of a man with his 'tribe'.

The mountain road from Nyeri to Meru was scenic; a kaleidoscope of geographical features for tourists and administrators alike, so without a description my journey would be incomplete. If Nyeri and Nanyuki were the usual one-horse towns, Meru was even smaller and the proverbial horse had surely at 1800 shillings. (20 shillings to the pound). No tears were shed when it was left behind for the price originally paid.

As I've just mentioned, a transfer in those distant days was conducted with a certain degree of civility and not confined to an overnight flit. In this instance, I had to get to the other side of the mountain via Nanyuki Sports Club polo field and three hotels that I can't fail to mention in detail; so let's hit the road and begin the journey. From Nyeri, there are 7 miles of twisting roads to reach Kiganjo before the open plains flow towards Nanyuki. The Ndorobo horizon is then on your left as the last valley dips into Nanyuki Town, which is a single wide road with trading shops on either side; forget to slow down and you'll miss it completely. Exit Nanyuki, cross the Timau slopes and the Northern Frontier District (NFD) fills the eye as far as you can see; examine the haze and the imagination runs wild. Somalia, Sudan and Ethiopia are somewhere out there, a clear day is all that's needed. It's now plain sailing into Kinoru Division with Wason Timber on your right, and Imenti Forest is there for the felling on the other side of the road. But before we go into the detail of Meru Town the history of the three hotels in Nanyuki must be recalled, each with their own intrigues.

The 'Silver Beck' in Nanyuki was just 200 yards off the main Nyeri road; its uniqueness is a silver line drawn at zero latitude across the bar-counter. The northern and southern hemispheres were clearly defined for you to play the game of drinking in the north and swallowing the last drop below the equator. From the bar to the bed was a considerable distance, but the only risk was too much beer, the emergency had died long ago.

Another establishment, the Sportsman's Arms, epitomises a 'living dangerously' experience with a leopard sighting adventure almost guaranteed to happen. The Leopard's Lair extension was designed to encourage a feline pose for the starry-eyed tourist. The Shamshudin family, veterans on the local scene, ran this unique enterprise after 'Tree Tops' was burnt down. On a typical outing, Shamshudin would lead the shaking tourists into the forest to the sound of a clicking bolt action from his elephant gun; just in case, who knows, danger might be lurking in the shadows. Details would then emerge about the ferocious maneating beasts and the time he got away, and the more the visitors shook, the more delighted he was; the tune of his clicking bolt never failed to deliver an awesome fear. Earlier in the day, the cook from the hotel had wedged a goat's leg in the fork of the leopard's favourite tree, a place of habit, where he rarely failed to dine and show his spots.

Princess Elizabeth had beaten the Mau Mau by a whisker when she spent the night at Tree Tops Lodge in 1952, just before they 'struck the match' that burnt it down. Such events are in retrospect and speculation, but there is no doubt she was a Princess when she ascended the Tree on that fateful night, to be Queen of England in the morning. Whether she had the traditional breakfast was not my privilege to know, but Prince Philip conveyed the news about the death of King George VI when she arrived at Sagana Lodge. She then flew to England to meet the challenge, and you the reader should worry not, she'll outlive us all.

'Mawingu', was the biggest of the three hotels; its imposing entrance remains original to this day. 'Mawingu' (clouds in Kiswahili) has changed ownership many times over the years and has now settled down as Mount Kenya Safari Club. But as Mawingu in the past, it was closely associated with film stars Bill Holden and Stephanie Powers who, on Holden's death, inherited his personal game ranch, which is thriving as I record this little bit of history. The likes of film stars Ava Gardiner, Frank Sinatra (married to Ava) and Clarke Gable who played the White Hunter in 'Mogambo' (The Greatest), are intertwined with the Mawingu intrigues. The snows alone on the summit of Kilimanjaro make the film 'Mogambo' well worth viewing, if only to see how low the snow line was away back then. And let's not forget Grace Kelly the future Princess of Monaco, another of the greats, and dare I say, a good kisser in the film. Should you choose to consult the visitors' list of regulars at the Mawingu, another book could stand on its own to describe their antics in Nanyuki, and their world achievements. But for the moment, such repartee would not be complete without 'a tune' from Bunny Allen, a Kenyan character with a red MGA to match the glitz of the Hollywood Stars; plus the rhetorical question that always hung over his head…'did you 'do it' with Ava?' It still remains a mystery, and your guess is as good as mine?

Before we venture further, I'm bound to issue a warning about a personal experience that rattled my bones on one occasion when I was travelling to Meru. Never stop to answer the 'call of nature' in the middle of the night near Imenti Forest and leave your car door open. Because, after doing just that, I smelt a close presence as I continued on my journey. Not only was this presence very real, but it was breathing down the back of my neck and peering over my shoulder, its eyes on the road ahead. And to cap it all, the face in the rear view mirror had beady eyes and a dog-like snout, and it was even more hairy than I, in my younger days. I stopped, jumped out and shouted, and the baboon took off into the night. It was a terrifying experience for us both; he could well have jumped out of his skin as my bones continued to rattle!

At last we're almost there, so slow down and trickle into Meru Boma (town) from the forest road. Take the first turning to the right past the squash court, just above the new Police Officer's Mess. We're almost in 1957 and there's plenty of space with a splendid view over the golf course towards the town in the distance. Continue along the circuit road and you'll end up at the DC's office, but not before passing the DC's house and his guesthouse, where eventually, I lived for over 2 years. In the first instance I lodged at the 'Pig and Whistle' as I waited for the housing committee to make one of their 'lightening' decisions; so once again like Nyeri, I had been in the fortunate position of a single man with catering facilities provided in hotel style. Tilley lamps were the source of all light after dark in Meru, and the hot bath water came from a 44-gallon drum, under which a fire was lit courtesy of the trees from Imenti forest.

Much to my delight, I had linked up with a new aquaintence in Meru, who was due to share in my boma crimes over the next 2 years. Harry Kerridge was a person of small stature who always wore settler shorts, ankle socks, and a big smile to confront his daily rigours. Sympathetic blue eyes and vibrant humour were among his best features, and he was also staying at the Pig with a similar status to mine. On occasion, we would walk the length of the golf course swinging a club to prove we knew what the game was all about; the clubhouse bar was in our sights. Harry was running the Administration Tribal Police and Transport and had just completed a contract with the Rio Tinto copper mines in Chile. In his 40s, he had collected a wealth of experience to promote his good guy image, which came along with fluent Spanish from his South American days. Eventually, we shared a cottage in one of the smallest corners of Meru Boma; the DC's guesthouse in the DC's garden to be precise. Empty for years, it had suddenly become available to save the hotel subsidy paid from the travelling vote. We were not best pleased by such an action and renovations were at our expense. Unlike the 21st century where luxury flows and government pays, if the present daily papers are telling the truth.

Harry and I lived in that guesthouse for the next two years, during which time an Alsatian dog by the name of 'Burridge' was adopted. The name, a pun on Kerridge, was suggested by Bernard Shaw, and as we couldn't think of an alternative to Burridge, he was duly called Burridge and that was that. My previous boss in Nyeri was another name conundrum entirely; he was also a Bernard Shaw like the one in Meru, which suggests the name game by design was to follow the famous. Encouraged by G.B.S., playwright, critic, literary giant.

I kept in touch with Bernard long after our encounter in Meru, where the dear chap was chasing a General Service Medal when we were first met. Nick-named the 'Colorado beetle' to match its black and yellow ribbon, this medal was dished out to loyalists by the government in emergency areas. Much to his chagrin I declared I had been awarded two, one for my Nyeri campaign and another for Meru, to leave him even more distressed than ever. Whether he succeeded in getting just one I never knew, though I felt rather good with my name inscribed on the edge of two to Bernard's discomfort; it was never mentioned again. Nevertheless, medal or not, we met up in England where he was managing a boring Building Society on leaving the service. It was a steady humdrum job after Meru, but by then he was married and had a son. By chance and out of the blue, he confided in me that he enjoyed married life of a Sunday morning, before or after church I never knew, but now we're talking history and it matters not; he's with the Meru crowd in company of the angels, all good men and true. The administration housing was occupied entirely by Europeans in '57. I cannot recall any African senior staff, and to invent a different scenario to paint a more pleasing picture is not in my nature. In fact, the only African in authority was the District Assistant in charge of North Imenti Division, and he was living in Kinoru, not the town. His name was Silas M'Mugambi, a lovely man by any standards, and he alone pioneered his unique position among the Europeans. Eliphas Mburia, was another African of consequence who stood out from the crowd as Secretary to the Meru African District Council. He was running the Council affairs where I was obliged to count the money on a weekly basis, before Macdonald turned up from Scotland to check the books; quite frankly, with a name like that he couldn't aspire to come from anywhere else. He promptly fell in love with the local Community Development Officer Dorothy Green, whom I guess he'd swept off her feet to eventually marry. But in the meantime I'm pleased to report he relieved me of my duties and embraced the ADC as their Financial Adviser.

An unusual incident springs to mind as I vividly recall Kinoru without too much affection; it concerns the local stadium soon after my arrival in the district. During one of my weaker moments I agreed to referee a championship match between two local teams, the Community Development Officer Mike Seaward was indisposed. Much to my credit, so I was told, my name had been mentioned as an unbiased type of person and that's why I was asked to perform the referee's duties. Not because they couldn't find anyone else; well that's what I was led to believe, and when someone said it was a pat on the back for me, who was I to argue? So a coin was flipped and the kick-off was like any other, by half-time the score was 1-1. A five-minute interval and the second half got underway; the mystery of the match was about to happen. The ball was booted into the crowd and we waited for its return, but the crowd returned no ball at all. Amazingly it had vanished, disappeared in a fraction of a second, not to be thrown back. I would solve the matter when the match was over, but in the meantime, I used a well-worn replacement ball. Finally the match ended in a draw, no shoot-outs in those days. To find the missing ball a serious search was undertaken by the Tribal Police, using a certain amount of brutality to turn the crowd inside out and nothing came to light. The mystery of the ball that had disappeared was never solved, but by then I had been in Kenya for a couple of years and the strangest of things were always happening; this event in Kinoru didn't dispel my thinking.

We return now to the Police Mess on the corner and take the straight road down the hill towards the DC's office. The Police Mess is on the right with a couple of Asian quarters on the left. The first is occupied by F.N.X. D'Mello my brilliant cashier, and Ali Khan the crafty court clerk in-charge of the government furniture in addition to his court duties, is the next house down. So I suppose, it came as no surprise when he was found to have 'borrowed' a senior-staff paraffin fridge from the stores for his own personal use.

Keeping to the left, the next building down the hill is the secondary school, commonly referred to by those in the know as 'St Foot's'. It was Keith Foot's calling to pontificate there of a Sunday, and if the singing was anything to go by, it was a popular gathering. Primarily, Keith was a D.O. of good standing and a person with high connections in British society. And if I may draw an analogy here, he was akin to a poor Sir Evelyn Baring, the Governor who was known to balance the books at Government House with a personal cheque should he over-spend. Keith was also a man of private means who didn't need to rely on his DO's salary, and John Cumber who knew of this, treated Keith with a certain amount of awe. Sir Hugh Foot, the Cyprus Governor appointed by Harold Macmillan at the time of Enosis, (Union with Greece) was a connection loosely mentioned by Keith on one occasion. When he purchased a new white Mercedes 180 in '58 using his private means he took me for a spin on the rugged Meru roads to leave me yearning for a similar carriage. Little did I imagine at that time that I would meet Stella his future wife, who was staying at the YWCA before they married. Fortunately, and unfortunately, the last time I met Keith was just before his fatal road accident. He was shopping in Nakuru at the time for his farm in Molo and looking extremely well, his quadruple bypass was behind him and the firmness of his handshake hadn't diminished one bit. Elgon Court, three little boys, a laughing Stella from Kakamega and a wry smile from Keith are some of the memories I will always treasure. Today, I have a quadruple bypass myself and regard Keith as my pioneer.

Further down the road turn right and cut across the lower side of the DC's office and you will be in front of the local jua-kali garage, (hot sun, hadn't really been coined in those days to describe a hotchpotch enterprise or entrepreneurial worker) under the management of John Simons. It was but a few yards before the top of the High Street with the most famous shop in town. Mohamed Moti & Sons, who were trading in Meru in 1908, before the colonial government arrived on the scene. Deservedly, it was also the largest shop and overshadowed a collection of tiny maduka (shops) squeezing a meagre living to survive. Finally, at the bottom of the high street the two big banks were operating in a very small way; the Standard was the first to set up shop with Noel Brownhill at its helm and

Barclays then 'climbed out of bed' to establish a branch several years later. Kianjai, the Nyambenes and Maua were put on the map by the London Somali refugees, who had fled their once beautiful land blessed with Italian architecture and a gifted people, now struggling to survive in a world that 'owes' them a living. Their future remains to be seen, but foreign exchange from London to pay for miraa exports was good news for Kenya.

Should you by chance fail to stop in Meru High Street you may find yourself on the main road travelling towards Chuka, via Kathita Division on the river by the same name; it is also the beginning of the mountain track to climb Kenya. Twenty more bends and Nkubu remains further afield as you stop at Egoji, a place amounting to practically nothing. On reflection, I have to admit that's not quite true, because something did happen in Egoji to lift it from the mundane for those on the spot at the time. The party in progress was celebrating Alan Jones's birthday. Alan, or Al as he was known, was a talented linguist who had spent an exciting National Service career listening to Russian radio chatter in Berlin, and to end up in Egoji was the end of the world for him. Anyway, whatever the idiosyncrasies, many guests turned up to celebrate, and were in the right place at the right time to enjoy the warmth from a memorable fire! The party got off to an explosive start as the trip-wire flares lit the road leading up to the house; a thoughtful clown had also placed some thunderflashes in the outside toilets to shift any signs of constipation! The house where we gathered was designed and built by Al, using minimal materials. A low stonewall with offcuts to ceiling level was covered by a thatched grass roof; an extensive building by any standards and government furniture was provided. When the first spark ignited, there must have been some 20 vehicles within the barbed wire compound, the beer was flowing and the meat was fizzling; it was clearly an all-man show with women's lib still in the shadows, so rowdy behaviour with crude jokes was the norm.

A puff of smoke appeared from the roof and no one paid much attention; then all of a sudden we had a raging fire on our hands and Jones took charge; after all it, was his birthday and his house, but by the time the flames began to leap, there was nothing we could do to put them out. But all was not lost that evening, it was cold and the guests appreciated the warmth from the flames, but that's as far as the good side got. With no rain clouds in the sky we turned our attention to the things of value in the house besides Jones's clothes, bearing in mind the government furniture might have to be paid for if we didn't save a few sticks. The cost of the house came from petty cash and a lot of ingenuity, so nothing on that score was accountable. It therefore followed that the rest of the evening was devoted to the contents, and in particular a government bed for Jones to sleep on that very night. A wardrobe full of his clothes then followed the bed before the guests were drained of their good intentions, to adopt a more leisurely pace of their own volition.

In the end, everyone had enjoyed a scintillating evening in the presence of the fire, and the drinking of beer from a 'ringside seat' was seen as a life-time experience. Naturally, the DC was not informed about this burning event and his District Intelligence Committee remained blissfully ignorant of the tragedy, which had at last, put Egoji on the map. I'm pleased to report that I attended the re-opening of a brand new house on the same foundations but 2 months later, complete with the re-installed furniture. The business of cooking meat had been moved out of harm's way, to the bottom of the garden.

We now resume our journey from Egoji to Chuka with 20 miles of hairpin bends to the divisional HQ and Peter Dempster, the ginger-headed District Officer from the Emerald Isle. He was known as the DO who lived off his mileage claims and saved his salary for greater things to come; as the one to pay his claims I admired the extent of his travel and thrift. He had bought a Land Rover with a government loan in spite of an official vehicle being available at taxpayer's expense. Even back then, there were people who worked all angles with a smile at a shilling a mile, which was a fancy figure at the time.

Chuka Town is eventually reached through Chogoria Mission, regarded as the second capital of the district in the 50s. If you examine the graves in the cemetery there, you will see a space occupied by an elderly nun hacked to death by the Mau Mau in '53; they were looking for the day's collection. R.I.P. dear lady. By comparison, Chogoria is very much on a par with Tumu Tumu Mission in Nyeri District, but without the famous landmark hill. However, should you forget to apply your brakes on reaching Chuka you are likely to end up in Embu Town; host to the famous Izaak Walton Inn, a paradise for bird watchers and fly fishermen; it was named after the 'Father of Angling', whose book the 'Complete Angler' was first published in 1653 when the snows were deep on Kenya and only the surrounding tribes enjoyed the pleasure. That's what Embu is all about; rainbow trout and a fishermen's dreams to test his skills. To add spice to the adventure the half-doors in the guest rooms are a crowning feature, to let the breeze blow in and keep the animals out.

Now let's switch back to Meru town and bear a little bit

more to the right after the DC's office, where the Pig and Whistle lies and the Meru Sports Club is slightly further up the hill; a good place to be of an evening. This guided tour is far from complete and offers only a fleeting description of Meru history, in a place where I was honoured to lodge in '57, just before the greenery of the golf course became a housing project. The Provincial Commissioner Eastern Province didn't like the 'colonial' game and contrived to thwart the up and coming Kenya golfer's; a strange type of justice then prevailed when his family excelled in the very same sport he so despised. Eluid Mahihu was a friend of long standing from our first encounter in Kitale, where he took over as DC from Peter Shiyukah. Our association stretched from the time of his new water-tank in Mathira, to the PCs water-map in his Embu garden where we took tea. My house in Lower Hill Road Nairobi was another occasion when we met up; he was building on State House road next to the Bishop's residence and posed a few questions, but Eluid being Eluid, had a mind of his own, and rarely took any advice he asked of me.

8

John Cumber was a charming unflappable gentleman who was always in control; at 6 feet plus he surveyed all those he met from the top of the head to their toes, but because of his height he usually stooped to engage in conversation. Clean shaven, his blue eyes and fresh complexion supported a well balanced if slightly pointed nose and his smile was pleasantly surprising. John was the District Commissioner Meru; a 'salt of the earth' was the expression he usually used to describe other people, and he was truly a 'salt-of-the-earth' himself. He could never say no, which resulted in several people claiming the same house when it was promised many times over. His dear wife Margaret raised two sons who joined the Gurkha Regiment, to tread the same path as their father with army war service in India. Before John finally left the colonial service he was private secretary to Governor Patrick Rennison and the politically spiced Malcolm McDonald, Kenya's first and last Governor General. From my Meru guesthouse days I had access to the State House swimming pool when I stayed over in Nairobi with John and Margaret, for which I will be ever grateful. I believe the pool has since disappeared. After Independence John landed a job with 'Save the Children Fund', and with Princess Anne as his patron, Sir John Cumber came about, to conclude a colourful career.

Glyn Hughes, another great, was born in Tanganyika and held the position of District Officer 1 in Meru when I first arrived; his good lady was called Dot or Dorothy, the choice was yours. Glyn was a talented Kiswahili speaker and one of the few able to write Kiswahili in Arabic script. One of his proclivities was to think up high-flying English words to flummox the ignorant such as me, and to ask their meaning made his day. He kindly tested me gently for the standard oral Kiswahili examination within the two-year period before my annual increment was blocked; that was the rule in those days. On retirement from the Colonial Service, Glyn joined MI5 with a desk on the banks of the Thames in conjunction with Charing Cross station. Naturally, no one knew for sure about his hush-hush employment, which left only one thing for certain about Glyn; he would be writing reports with difficult words on a higher plane to bamboozle the British establishment, the wananchi (inhabitants) of Whitehall.

The African District Council collected taxes in parallel with the GPT (graduated personal tax). Which was a central government tax that varied from Shs.20 p.a. to Shs.200. It was based on one's affluence; though Shs.20 was the standard acceptable charge and rarely challenged when collected in the field. Quite frankly, noone was going to ask anyone to fill in thousands of declaration forms for an army of clerks to make assessments; for once the government had got it right. The top man in the ADC, as I mentioned, was Eliphas Mburia the Council Secretary, and I am told Jackson Angaine some time in the past was also a power in the same council, but that was a detail he never discussed with me when he became my boss as the Minister of Lands in 1966. By then, Angaine was known as the 'King of Meru' and was adored by another grand old man, Kenyatta himself. Age-mates and twins in many ways, describes them well.

'Sir,' as I always addressed Angaine during my tenancy in Lands, would sometimes reminisce about when he was a youth and first left home to look for work in 'the city', which according to him was Meru town a few miles from his home. I asked him in which year that would be and he couldn't recall, but he told me he landed his first job as a cook in the house of the Maize Marketing Board Manager, an Englishman by the name of Benson. I had a feeling his first job was that of a houseboy and he had promoted himself to cook immediately, when in fact he'd been promoted to cook by Benson after his hidden talents were discovered, but who knows the answer to that?

"Mr Palmer," he always called me Mr Palmer.

"When I worked for Mr Benson I could never understand the way he loved his little dog so much. I know you will ask me how I knew about his love for his little dog, so let me explain. Mr Benson had an old safari car with open sides and a wooden box-body with two comfortable seats in the front, and a wooden toolbox bench-seat in the back without a cushion. Can you imagine?" Angaine seemed to pause and reflect on the hardness of the toolbox before he continued.

"Can you imagine?" were the enquiring words Angaine always used, when he wanted to solicit sympathy for some injustice he may have endured.

He then continued. "That wooden toolbox without a cushion was very hard, and Mr Benson told me that was my seat when we went on safari. He would then put his little dog in the comfortable passenger seat beside him. This happened time and time again, so I had to ask him how he could put a dog in a comfortable seat in his car and make me sit on a hard wooden box when I was a human being, and after all, a dog is only a dog. And these are the very words he used to reply to my question."

"Jackson, in my view that little dog means more to me than any human being, so I have to look after him. That's why I put him in the front with me, I hope you understand?"

"Mr Palmer, how can I understand why you Europeans treat your animals better than human beings?" Angaine threw the question over to me.

"Perhaps, they are more loyal than human beings?" I suggested. To which Angaine replied, "Hmm," to wrap up his thinking on what was a prickly subject to him.

On another occasion, Angaine wanted to vent his feelings about his current driver's conduct, so he summoned me to his office. After all, I was the Assistant Secretary Finance and Personnel, and the personnel part of my job description was always to his liking. In this particular instance, it had precipitated the employment of a certain nominated young man to be his driver. The same young man had now got himself into a spot of trouble, and I was to hear about his bad driving 'skills'. As usual, I was never offered a chair to hear his tale of woe, so I stood before his desk for the story to unfold.

"Mr Palmer, my vehicle was in an accident on the way to my farm." He waited for his words to make an impression.

"I'm sorry to hear about that Sir, are you alright?"

"Yes, but as a Minister of the government I was shamed in

a very bad way by my driver," his words exactly.

"How can I be of assistance Sir; what happened, and what did he do?"

"To avoid an oncoming lorry he went off the road and turned my car upside-down on its roof. I then had to crawl through the back window with all the villagers watching. The primary school children then started clapping and jumping up and down when I finally stood up. Imagine that? A Minister squeezing through the back passenger window of his own car because the door was jammed, then there was all this clapping."

"I'm sorry to hear that Sir," I took a firm hold on my senses and controlled my smile, "the driver has clearly misbehaved and he has to go. Would you please tell him to hand in his uniform and I'll get you a replacement." Uniforms were passed from one employee to the next in days of old; that was the system, bugs and all and money was saved. Today they wear suits like their bosses, to play at bosses when their bosses are not in sight. How times have changed.

"Mr Palmer, normally I would agree he has to go, but I have a small problem here because he's my wife's relative, so I have to give him another chance, but I want this to be on his record and that's why I called you in."

The moment I closed Angaine's door the count down began to the next driving event. It had to happen and it wouldn't be long before another bunch of school children were jumping up and down with enough glee to give Angaine the courage to face the wrath of his wife. How the driver managed to stage a similar accident to the one before, no one could imagine, but that's exactly what he did; the guy had hidden talents. "Mr Palmer, that driver has to go!" were the words I heard after a second detailed account of his crawling through another car window, believed to be even smaller than the first. Once again he had struggled under the watchful eyes of a bunch of primary school kids, and true to form they clapped their hands in delight and jumped up and down when he stood up. His audience had come out of the woodwork like they always did, drawn by the noise of the crash.

Each month I would travel throughout the district from Chuka to Tharaka, Maua and Miathene in the Nyambenes. I paid the wages in cash to all the Administration staff, 300 plus in total. The printed pay-sheets would arrive in the Post from Nairobi with a cheque to be cashed at the local bank. It was usually in the region of Shs. 500,000, and to put this amount into perspective, a tribal policemen's pay was Shs.103.50 a month and a divisional clerk would earn Shs.265, about the same as a Sub-chief. A Chief's salary was Shs.300 plus, but all these amounts varied according to seniority. Money had value in those days; the best fillet steak cost 70 cts a pound and a whole kienyeji chicken was just over a shilling or less at the butcher's shop, a large loaf of white bread would weigh in at 17 cts.

The 'pay-train' or Landrover was guarded by two tribal policemen with ancient .303 rifles from World War II, an unarmed driver, and I'll throw in myself for good measure to fight off possible crooks, though I usually hadn't the time to pickup my pistol from the armoury. In all of my government service I cannot recall a government cash robbery where violence was used; old fashioned law and order ruled the day. The usual format for stealing was by switching carbon receipts to show under collections; a method hard to check when the receipt holder disappears into the crowd with a different original. Tax clerks travelled freely in their areas with black steel cashboxes secured to their bicycle racks by strips of rubber inner-tubes, which was the only barrier between the box and the highway-robber. Yes indeed, there were robberies all the time, but as I've just said, violence was rarely used. Showing guns and shouting 'hands up and deliver' was still in the realms of cinema audiences, and yet to come in the form of new modernday Kenya crooks. The crooks I personally came across during my time in the District Treasury were of a more devious nature, a forged signature or perhaps a difficult to identify thumbprint was the usual deception. Even a big toe 'thumb-print' had been found on one occasion to endorse a compensation cheque; how anyone knew the difference I never found out. Machakos district and Maasai-land were divided by the rail-track from Mombasa to Nairobi. For convenience, my office was the local compensation payout point to relatives of those run down by a noisy train travelling at 20 mph. It takes some believing, but it happened on a regular basis and Shs.2,400 was the going rate, but when these cheques were not collected an opportunity for 'diversion' was sometimes to tempting to ignore. The Mombasa railway line did not discriminate on a tribal basis; once on the track your life was at risk. In 1960 war broke out between the tribes when the Wakamba were spotted grazing their cattle on the Maasai side of the railway track. The administration interceded when herdsmen arrived at Machakos hospital with spears sticking through their guts. But well before then, the Wakamba on hearing the news hired Mercedes trucks to bear warriors with brand new bows and arrows towards the border. A small loss of life then prevailed before the Tribal Police were ordered to shoot at anyone crossing the track. The situation then returned to normal, for the taking of lives to be left to the trains.

My biggest phobia on pay-safaris was a request to borrow my pen for a newly found signing skill. For authenticity, the paying officer witnessed each printed pay sheet that usually contained a row of thumbprints, not signatures. Everyone knew everyone, ghost workers were just not there, and only a few genuine people ever missed these happy occasions. For the records and your interest, the going rate for my cook at that time was Shs. 100 per month and anything he could eat undetected. His pay was almost ten percent of my salary.

On one of my pay-safaris, Dick Cashmore, a newly arrived DO in Meru and the son of an English bishop no less, accompanied me to see the district where he was about to become the DO 1, replacing Peter Fullerton. During my time, Peter, a gangling intelligent fellow, even taller than John Cumber, sometimes voiced strange ideas from dizzy heights when on his feet at district meetings. One of his more bizarre suggestions I clearly recall, was for all colonial officers to have only one home leave after joining the service, after which they should settle down overseas on a permanent basis; he confirmed my thinking that lunatics were lurking in the shadows. At the beginning of this book I had joined the service with the promise of home leaves on a regular basis, so I didn't need to embrace such dumb suggestions that might catch on. Fortunately, they were never to see the light of day, but the very fact that they were voiced by a moderately responsible person had to shake one's thinking. Even my hard working clerk in Meru, Hezekiah Ogana, a gem from Nyanza, took 6 weeks home leave every 2 years, and the local staff that lived in Meru had the same privilege on their home ground. Those were the generous terms offered by the colonial government based on the fact that, land at home required supervision and the wife and children needed some family life. For sure, the wife and children would sometimes visit their spouses during the school holidays, but this was usually a costly exception, rather than the rule.

Dick Cashmore was known for his enquiring mind into local historical facts that kept him busy in addition to his administrative duties. As a thinker who noted the unusual, he was always in his element with unique off-the-cuff answers; he also played an excellent game of squash to whip the physical into shape. We became firm friends and much to his credit, he was one of the few bachelors who actually entertained guests to dinner. It usually took the form of a buffet supper, but the effort was there and far exceeded anything Harry or I could ever offer. Our diners only extended to the odd guest, and in addition to their oddness they had to like cottage pie. We went through a lengthy period of cottage pie whilst in Meru, after the roasted chicken was stopped when Harry began to act in bird-like ways. I have since met Dick in Richmond Surrey where he has a flat near the Crown Inn on the Richmond Road; near to my own area of town. The last time we collided was actually on Richmond Bridge, and I thank God that he was looking extraordinarily healthy on that occasion. But let me cast my mind back to our last Mombasa encounter just before Independence, and link his duties to that of historian checking the records, before I dwell on the most recent Mau Mau torture awards settled out of court in 2013.

The British government clearly accepted the fact that atrocities had been committed on both sides during the conflict some 60 odd years ago; as a result twenty million pounds changed hands with an out-of-court settlement to appease for the British sins. But this is not the end of matter and why should it be; when the Kikuyu nation is aroused for easy money, open-eyed and sticky fingered, other claims must surely follow. A queue to re-open the floodgates for a further forty thousand 'long suffering claimants' is gathering pace as I put pen to this paper. And the greedy UK lawyers are also gathering pace to squeeze the milk from the udder of a new 'Jersey cow'; a couple of squirts for their clients and a bucket full for themselves. Is there anyone else out there with dubious claims, the British government is dying to help?

Whilst I'm on the subject, another anomaly comes to mind; the foreign-aid industry in Britain is devised to squander the highest percentage to GDP of any country in the world. It's all part of their scheming to splurge British funds on dubious projects. Prime Minister Cameron inflicted this programme on the British public using his majority in parliament to ring-fence the 'fraud'. After which, Brexit is blocked by the same parliament ignoring a national referendum that wanted out of the European Union. Which begs the question, where is the sense for lavish overseas aid without a thought for the poverty back home. To hell with school meals, let the children starve and the homeless freeze to death, our international image is more important. The overseas aid fat-cats who throw tax-payer's money into the wind and hope it will disappear. A recent Ethiopian musical adventure of over $100 million is one example that came to light; absolute lunacy, before it was stopped, but who will be held to account for the original decision and wastage from the time it was first launched? More publicity is needed to squeeze their 'cojones'; whether they have them or not, these society leeches must be stopped!

Dick Cashmore, ex-Meru, was in Kenya for a specific reason prior to independence; he was charged with sifting through files to determine history as it actually was before the local historians get to tamper with the facts. I never knew what he did precisely and neither did he volunteer any information, but if it was his project it had to be an activity with good intentions, which begs the question. Did the British government use information collected by Dick to 'shoot themselves in the foot', or was such information harmless and not connected to the most recent torture trials? But whatever the answer, doubt remains; why would the Brits delight in crucifying themselves with another out-of-court settlement to enrich the lawyers, with a few crumbs for their clients. The year is 2015 and I have sadly heard of the recent demise of Richard Cashmore. I passed by his flat in Richmond Road and failed to get a reply, but the downstairs neighbour came to my rescue. Richard, among other things, had bequeathed his historic research to his old Cambridge College where the answers to some of these recent claims may be, but who would want to know, when the first tranch chickens have already flown the coop.

After the out-of-court settlement in 2013, one could be forgiven for thinking a few extra deserving cases were missed, but that was before the word got around. It now appears that 41,000 'long-suffering-souls' were left off the previous settlement; cast to test the 'waters'. I doubt we will ever know how many genuine claimants have appeared so far and how many impostors are trying their luck for those already in heaven, but the young in their mother's arms back then are now over 60 years old, and the only part they played at that time was wetting their pants and crying. Those who were 18 years in '52 and are still alive and kicking, must be few and far between and in their 80's plus today. Birth details were sketchy in the '40s and even if they were born at that time, they would have been but 12 or younger when the emergency was declared. And the government of that day, as evil as they were perceived to be, detained not children. The average life expectancy precludes most of the new 41,000 hopefuls, but be assured they're hopeful for another out-of-court settlement helped by those who want to keep their jobs in overseas aid.

I received a letter from the Foreign Office Legal Department in 2016, they had traced me as a person working for the Provincial Administration in Nyeri in 1955, an area of Mau Mau activity. Apparently, the Mau Mau were pushing their luck yet again, and wanted more compensation to match the last out-ofcourt settlement. And let's face it; they have a reasonable chance of success when the overseas administrators encourage such activities. Twice, I presented myself at the Foreign Office legal establishment at their request and we worked on a statement of some 20 pages. I also gave them a cine-tape about Nyeri made in 1955. Much time was involved and accepted by them without a thought for my welfare, except for a cup of coffee requested by me. Let me also recall my temerity to suggest a return airfare from Kenya.

"We don't pay witness expenses," was the curt reply. So I refused to sign my statement, but gave them the Nyeri tape for free as my civic duty to stop the UK from being rippedoff by the do-gooders in overseas aid. They needed some extra evidence to help them say no for a change! I have yet to hear of the outcome of this latest torture con brought by 41,000 'long suffering' people, but of one thing I am absolutely certain, another out of court settlement will be made in some form or other whatever the legal time-frame. Perhaps a clever land-scam will emerge to squeeze compensation from a different angle, to enrich the promoters with a couple of coins for the suffering? To get rid of overseas aid willingly assisted by the High Commission is the problem, but worry not, they'll manage with the help of the irresponsible staff who spend too much time in the 'mid-day sun'.

Principles and honesty rarely evolve when the aroma of money is detected; get your hands on as much as you can by any means possible is the norm; human nature was never designed to be selfless. One of the more popular reasons bandied around to justify compensation is the guilt felt by the ex-colonial masters who tortured freedom fighters, but whether or not they actually did who cares; it's the thought that counts and yields the cash. Aid money is therefore paid out on a regular basis to set the conscience free. And kid yourself not, the 'do-gooders in Britain' are on a role to take aid-money for themselves when they retire. What makes them what they are none can tell, but they're in league with the gluttonous lawyers, who slurp from a similar trough.

A typical example of American generosity that is usually taken for granted, was their unbelievable kindness when they helped thousands of Kenyans who claimed to be in the vicinity of the bomb when the U.S. Embassy was wrecked in 1998, which was really a question of national security and not the responsibility of US. The crowds on that day were spectacular and their numbers grew as they heard about the possibility of much compensation. And to the credit of the Americans, most claims if not too unreasonable, were accepted as genuine and paid to help the suffering, whatever the origin of injury.

Appeasement British style, with Mau Mau compensation this late in the day describes the present British dilemma. Chamberlain and Hitler made the word 'appeasement' famous in 1939, and it lives today with its teeth firmly gripping the butt of the British aid budget. Money can never right the wrongs of history, though it helps to sooth the wounds. Malaysia is now sniffing at the roots of the British money tree for others to follow; if the Kenya demands show a profit. Recently, a county government in Kenya budgeted for a shopping spree to London with an ulterior motive; to brief a team of British lawyers to sue on behalf of 100,000 family members from a long-dead Kipsigis generation. Growing tea over the years on Kipsigi land had offered jobs to millions of Kenyan's for the workers to pay taxes, what cunning devils these colonials were. Doubt not for a minute, Kenyans are nimble people and fleet of foot in any form and long distance running is their preference; so if they're lucky they will win this race whatever the challenge, and may the size of their prize match their 'brass' if their lawyers don't gobble it first.

A change of attitude to the Emergency was supervised in 2016 by a naive British High Commissioner, who proudly posed with a Mau Mau Shujaa, hero, for their picture to appear in the local press. The occasion was the unveiling of a £100,000 statue, paid by the British tax payer at the instigation of William Hague, the Foreign Secretary. It defies belief and stands alone in British history, as one of the strangest acts of all. The courageous women honoured by that statue had risked their lives to feed the Mau Mau in the forest, to give them the strength to kill their fellow Kenyans and the kith and kin of the British High Commissioner. Such a demonstration begs the question, to whom do the others appeal for compensation; the relatives of the helpless pregnant women and small children hacked to death in the Lari massacre of 1953?

On a more pleasant note, recent history reveals that some communicators during the Mau Mau days used a gigantic hollowed-out tree in the vicinity of Treetops as a letter box. The KGB (Russian secret service) with their ears and noses to the ground then heard about this innovation, to use the same idea in Hyde Park London during the cold war years. Unfortunately, such activities were not subject to patent by the Mau Mau, so lifegoes on and so must we, but the possibility still exists for a smart young Kikuyu to squeeze a shilling or two for the use of their original idea, launched in the Aberdare forest.

A memorable chapter during my stay in Meru was the opening of Meru Mulika Lodge; the Shifta menace was in full swing at the time and even with such turmoil the Adamsons' continued to live at Lara with the new lodge nearby. Elsa and her lion cubs were their best friends. On occasion they would hit the headlines in Meru Boma with a full grown lion in the back of their truck, much to the delight of a fearful crowd.

My final epitaph in Meru was in solid form for all to see; my tongue-in-cheek activities to develop the Golf Club extension in the shortest time possible. A new servants' quarter next to the clubhouse was my objective, with a budget of a thousand shillings and a load of prisoners who enjoyed getting out and about, but today it's called slave labour. Cement was purchased and free stone was quarried; the iron window frames doing nothing at the Ministry of Works were also sneaked into the equation. When all these ingredients were eventually put together, a new construction cast shadows upon the Meru skyline. Who built such a colossus without planning permission consensus questioned, and I raised my hand to take the blame. In fact, the building was so large that the DC could see it from his office window, sufficiently so, to get 'Prince Charles' type comments about the 'carbuncle' on the Meru skyline. Were such comments reasonable or over the top I really didn't know, but whatever the position I enjoyed being the cause of dubious debate. My building belittled the clubhouse; very grand and morally wrong perhaps, but ego building for me, nevertheless.

John Cumber was never one to be daunted by a change on the Meru skyline; it didn't phase him one bit, and as a true salt of the earth he would sort out the 'carbuncle' problem with a minimum of disruption. The Ministry of Work's man who hailed from South Africa was duly summoned and told what John had in mind to do, about the staff quarters built by me. 'That up there', he pointed, 'blighting the Meru skyline'. Don't pull it down he was quick to add, but build a new and bigger clubhouse to put the servants quarters back in the shade. It must be at least three times the size of that 'carbuncle', he again pointed up the hill through his office window. And that's about it, the history of the new Meru Sports Club in '59. If it hasn't been grabbed since then by land developers, it must still be there as a colonial relic to mark John Cumber's Administration, which also places me there in bricks and mortar, as the guy who fired his endeavours.

9

1957 came and went, and so did a very important step in Kenya's history. The first 8 African members were elected to serve in the Kenya Legislative Council; don't hold your breath, but even I was eligible to vote for this once-in-a-lifetime experience. The number of votes was determined by one's personal qualifications, which resulted in the eking out of voting powers in dribs and drabs to elect the first African members. One man one vote was not the rule in '57; the maximum number of votes permitted was four per person, with a different coloured card to match the number recorded in the voters roll. It was easy, simple and straightforward, and no one was allowed to challenge the democracy of such an unequal system; the colonialists were running the show and that was that, no discussion allowed. To settle the matter I was issued with a blue card to cast four votes; my first and last voting effort in Kenya

Inside the polling station was a line of boxes with symbols such as a Lion, Giraffe or Lantern, to attract your vote for the candidate of your choice. It was all planned to help the voters master their first time experience; if they couldn't read they would recognize the symbol. Politics and dirty tricks go hand in hand, and this first time election was no exception. In fact, one challenging candidate was heard to smear an opponent's reputation by twisting a symbol to mean no good. He made an example of the 'Lantern', which if voted for, would burn much paraffin at the voters expense to light the dark future they were sure to get. For the record, there were no women reps in those early days. A seperate book could be written on the twists and turns to squeeze the gullible in favour of an exponent; the Kenyan politician was born to invent the invention, the mind has to boggle at the thought! On the actual day, the election had run a smooth course. The boxes were duly sealed at the close of business, and much like my third and final experience in Baringo District in '63, nothing had been too complicated, but by then, one person, one vote, was the rule.

Yes indeed, I had managed to get 4 votes, which had been the maximum number allocated to any one person from evidence produced on registration. At the time of voting you would be rechecked against the register to receive a ballot card of a corresponding colour to the number of votes you were allowed to cast for one candidate only. I was given a blue card representing my 4 votes; education, income, age, and the very fact that you were there. Bernard Mate, was my choice that day. As a Meru man he was one of our foremost characters in Central (Province) constituency. A humble person with no modern day pomp, he felt for others and was duly elected. As a matter of interest, the 8 African representatives finally elected to the Kenya Legislative Council in 1957 were Tom Mboya - Nairobi, Ronald Ngala - Coast, Oginga Odinga - Central Nyanza, who received the most votes of any candidate, Daniel Arap Moi - Rift Valley, Masinde Muliro - North Nyanza, Lawrence Oguda - South Nyanza, James Muimi - Ukambani, and finally my chosen man Bernard Mate - Central, who lived in Meru District.

Election Day in Miathene began at 6 am; the ballot boxes with symbols marked on their sides had been placed behind a privacy curtain the day before, so my first duty was to make sure the boxes were still empty before we started. The voting procedure was simple; after the name was checked a voters card was issued to correspond with the number of votes entitled; it was then up to the voter to place the card in the ballot box of their choice, no division of votes was possible. Agents were permitted within 20 yards of the booth and vocal campaigning in the immediate area was barred. All in all, it had been an uneventful day; no riots, not much excitement and the polling station closed at 6 pm. The full ballot boxes were then loaded onto the Land Rover and taken to Meru for counting. A single tribal policeman with an ancient rifle represented our security; a couple of clerks and myself was the team. For my efforts I pocketed Shs.200. The measly 200 bob was top of the range back then, until the mouth-watering allowances pioneered today by the new elite began to bite. All told, it had been an exciting event for some and a brand new life lay ahead for a few, but boma life in my little world all of my own remained unchanged; the rhythm reverted to normal.

Once a month all the heads of departments in the district were invited to gather around and discuss their mutual problems. John Cumber the district boss chaired the gathering in his office; he wanted to know what was going on, and from time to time when the meeting closed, he was actually fully informed. And as a matter of custom and to ease the pain, tea and imported biscuits from England were sparingly served at his expense. Fortunately for the low life such as I, the DC's secretary took the notes on these occasions for leaks to become juicy facts. Edward Snowden and WikiLeaks had yet to learn from us. And by the way, fingers didn't glide over keyboards back then, they punched mechanical contraptions.

The District Medical Officer David Harland was a man with a throaty laugh, horn rimmed spectacles and a full head of straight brown hair parted to one side. He was usually of good humour, but what he had to report on this occasion was far from amusing to him. Some anti-social activities had been detected in Marimanti to relieve a certain boredom in life, which in the end had required his medical skills to prise buckshot from backsides; the District Assistants were running amok. He felt his time could be better spent in other ways and asked the DC to put a stop to a dangerous game. Bert Shillinglaw the District Assistant in Marimanti had come all the way from bonny Scotland to work in Meru District; he was looking for excitement in life and had abandoned his dental mechanics to take up residence in the African bush. To those who knew him well, it came as no surprise to hear he was the brainless man behind such nonsense, about which the good doctor complained.

Bert was one of those people who enjoyed the uncertainty of playing with live explosives from the administration stores; life was dull and it was difficult for him not to touch the stock. Such items, for no particular reason, had been left lying around for years and were eventually to be his undoing. His intention to clear the flies from a 30 ft 'long-drop' toilet, was in mind as he withdrew a phosphorus grenade from his stores. How such evil munitions were in the government stores at that time is unthinkable, but for some reason phosphorus grenades were freely available in 1958.

Phosphorus explosions in a long-drop toilet full of flies

meant a lot of dead flies; no doubt about it. But when Bert pulled the pin and dropped the grenade into the depths the 7-second fuse held on to the action due to the age of the stock, but the answer to that we will never know for certain. Unfortunately, tragedy struck at around ten seconds when Bert was looking down the hole due to the delay. After the accident a burns specialist was summoned at John Cumber's insistence and no effort was spared to save Bert's eyes; his hands and face also healed a few months later with little scarring. I am pleased to report I received a Christmas card from Bert declaring his eyes to be OK and he was back to normal; as normal as he'd ever been. By then he had a job on his home turf as Secretary to the Scottish Lifeboat Institution and as there have been no headlines in the National Press about Bert and the drama he usually courted, I assume he's settled down to a normal life in Scotland, something he avoided in Meru. As it so happened that Christmas card was the last I heard from this colourful gentleman; lock up the matches if he's around!

Now let's return to David Harland's complaint and the fact that he didn't like wasting time removing buckshot from bums, and how the bums became peppered with shot in the first place. The idea behind the game devised by Bert was to avoid getting shot; since getting shot is painful, even with the smallest of grains. The 'motivator' in Marimanti was blindfolded, held a loaded shotgun and stood in an open space surrounded by thickets. The name of the game was 'KUKU' (chicken) according to Bert. It was designed to relieve the dullest of minds in the dullest of places. Several heroic admin. guys would lurk behind thick bushes and shout kuku! The blindfolded shooter then fires a shot in the direction of the sound, but by then everyone is bending down behind the bushes with their backs towards the man with the gun. Whether anyone is hit or not, heart beats are racing and adrenaline is high, that's what it's all about; living on the edge in Mariamanti. If no one is hit, the shooter changes places with one of the targets, another round is slipped into the breach for the game to continue until a loser has to visit the 'quack' (David Harland.)

Mind you, not everything was violent in Marimanti, Tharaka Division. For instance, the semi-scrub terrain projected a certain culture to make life good for the bachelors; a daily scene by design and not by chance. The locals were always strolling by to the delight the randy chaps staring from the DO's house, built to overlook the watering-hole. The lucky few who downed a beer on that porch around sundown, were by intention there to appreciate the pageant. Tall, topless, super magnificent, is the only way to describe such breasts that shamed the figure of the Venus de Milo in the Paris Louvre; their arms in addition were warm, to hold you tight.

The one and only Mount Kenya attracted day trippers in the 50's if your boots were on the ground in Meru. Harry Kerridge my buddy, suggested we make the effort and take a day-trip up the mountain; I was in good shape and the idea matched my energy. On the appointed day our Land Rover puffed and panted up the Kathita track to an altitude of 12,000 ft, and from there we hiked to the edge of the Lewis Glacier; an energetic walk describes it well, age was on our side. The whole event transpired something like this; the trees at 12,000 ft were covered in a 'witch-brew cobweb fashion', scientifically known as lichen. We then followed the Rhino tracks through the forest dodging fresh droppings, the askaris led the way. The tufts of grass as you emerge from the forest edge is a fairyland all of its own, and by then our final objective, the Lewis Glacier is on the skyline and clearly in sight; it even looked smooth from that distance, but when we eventually touched the first ice-edge it was rough, several feet high, jagged and rather dirty. But having come this far in just a few hours from the forest edge, we struggled to mount the glacier and stand atop. It made our day. Batian peak, named after the famous Maasai Laibon, mystique healer and medicine man, was another project entirely. It was 2,000 feet higher up and impossible to climb without ropes, much time and special clothes. But whatever our position, it had been a magnificent experience and enough to last a lifetime. Modesty prevents me from telling a different tale to claim the scaling of Batian in '57. I missed it by a few feet, several thousand to be precise, and I'm the first to admit it.

Meru, beautiful Meru, I could dwell on the subject forever, but with home leave beckoning and the object of my original adventure to Africa about to be fulfilled, my heart was light when I boarded the 'Caledonian' flight at the new Embakasi airport; UK was but hours away and Machakos was on the horizon when I returned.

10

The first home leave after 3 years 3 months offered a period of relaxation; 5 months with my feet up in the UK. A deposit was placed and payments arranged for my first investment in bricks and mortar; my mother Alice needed somewhere to live and so would I on my next home leave. My first tour of duty had been trimmed by 6 months to take up the position of District Revenue Officer in Machakos, and who was I to complain about home leave coming early. At last, after a lot of planning, my foot was on the 'long leave ladder' like my brother and father before him. My position in life could loosely be described as having arrived; the bonus was a government loan for a VW beetle on home-leave delivery. On landing at Heathrow I collected the car for shipment to Kenya at the end of my stay. The total package was £615, equivalent to East African Shs.12,300 at 20 to the pound; KGG 12 was the final result. Imagine my delight with a first new car and something I had never expected so soon in life; I blessed my lucky stars.

Halfway through my first tour I was granted a local leave of 14 days, which I put to good use; join me on my first African safari to Zanzibar. The second-hand Ford Consul with a front bench seat, a steering column gear-change and a radio as an extra, was still lacking the screen washers and heater when manufactured in 1955. And it was no nearer to completion when I sold it in 1959 to Larry Wateridge, of Sagana Falls to Lamu fame. Nevertheless, KBW 885 will always remain a sweet memory, 'old is gold' when I reminisce about that journey from Meru to Dar es Salaam on murram roads in '58. Wheel chains were carried for traction in mud, and I was bound to use such props to save 'my bacon' when the heavens opened and I found myself in a lake just after the tarmac at MacKinnon Road. The point where you think Mombasa I'm here, when there's another 100 miles to go! (See picture, my watery isolation MacKinnon Road.)

The Mombasa road in 1958 provided a modern day adventure much less challenging than Galton-Fenzi would have you believe in 1926. If you examine his records chiselled in stone next to the General Post Office, No.29 Kenyatta Avenue, you'll find it took them days to travel the distance now covered in hours. Nevertheless, whatever the brevity and hazards of my 5-hour trip, the wayside events were a first time for me and I enjoyed the ride immensely. Many regrets, you weren't sitting beside me.

Just outside Nairobi you are bound to cross the Mombasa railway line, (the duty free zone today) a bump bump affair over the railway and under the bridge of that time. The on-going construction of the new Embakasi Airport is then on your left. Next in line is the near death experience from the smell of the Kenya Meat Commission. It hits you hard, before you breatheeasy on the Athi river bridge with the twisted iron railings to save drivers from dropping over the edge. Stony Athi is then but a few yards ahead, and you quickly learn why it's called stony as you leave the smooth bridge crossing. I suspect it was all part of the plot to teach your car a lesson; speed is then of the essence to fly over the rocky-white surface towards Lukenya hills. After which, you pass the turn-off towards Machakos town on your left; to be my next District, though I didn't know it at the time. It was also the site-to-be for the first Kenya Capital if a lack of water hadn't changed the plan. Lest I have misled you, we are still on the Mombasa road and miles and miles of the Athi plains lie ahead; in fact they were so expansive I tapped the gauge to make sure the tank was full at shs.4 a gallon, or less than one shilling a litre in 1958. Ranch-land then lay ahead to occupy my all round vision with ever-changing murram colours from one hillcrest to another; they mesmerised my thinking. I had quickly learned a trick or two since setting out from Nairobi… don't let the car behind over-take or it'll push the dust through your door cracks, the ones you didn't know existed. It was a crying shame and a fact indeed; many a death came about by driving into a dust cloud just before overtaking. Dongas, (dry river beds) were the favourite habitat of the biggest of the big 5 that littered the Mombasa road in those beautiful days when I knew I was lucky. Rhinos, elephants and zebras were magic to the eyes, not to mention the petrified trees with millions of years lying around forever. The giant baobabs also had a role to play on the way to Mombasa; standing guard on either side of the road they made sure you kept to the straight and narrow. The billowing dustclouds behind the car gave a sense of progress, though I had little time to look back when my destination lay hundreds of miles ahead.

Between Kibwezi and Mackinnon road, Mac's Inn stood proud; an oasis beckoning at 150 miles, the halfway mark to Mombasa. Mac, was the owner and manager all rolled into one. In 1964 I attended the re-opening of the rebuilt premises; an ornate swimming pool had been added and a second floor extension offered roof top viewing; the name had also been changed to 'Tsavo Inn'. As luck would have it, I was on my way to catch the SS Uganda on home leave when the opening celebrations were in full swing as I passed by on the Mombasa road. Mzee Kenyatta had a long standing affinity with Tsavo Inn Mtito Andei, due to his dislike of flying combined with his love of the road to meet his people. It was also the halfway mark on his journey to Bamburi Beach for a view of the sea and some relaxation; tribal dancing had always been his fancy. Much into the future, some of his Ministers were heard to mention Mzee and his tribal dancing groups at Bamburi Beach. Strangely, or perhaps it wasn't so strange, it was all about the colour of their money and how to avoid attending such performances without causing Mzee's displeasure. Their objection was the payment of a small fortune if they were present, because when the performance ended Mzee would ask did you liked the dancing, to which they had to say 'yes'! So how could they refuse when told by Mzee to give a 'tip', the size of which was duly noted. The whole charade was becoming quite painful with the emptying of their pockets for future favours not yet in their plans. If I may coin an expression here, their fists were 'Kikuyu tight', but not tight enough for the prising hands of Jomo Kenyatta.

Before you reach Voi, land of the ruby and tsavorite gem stones acquired by the influential after independence, you will see Manyani Prison camp built in colonial times and much improved after independence; a desolate place describes it well. There's no doubt that the area was well chosen by the British, and remains a colonial monument to this day with a wealth of history retold just recently by the original Mau Mau inmates. Those who fought for independence and were tortured on this very spot. Voi Town, 20 miles further down the road is noted for its large war cemetery of numerous nationalities. The British War Graves Commission maintains it on a permanent basis via the DC's office Wundanyi. Some four years after my original Dar es Salaam safari, I subsequently stayed in Voi with Pam and Chris Benson, the district officer friend from Machakos, who was by then married with a brand new set of twins in 1962. Geoffrey Karithi was DC Wundanyi at the time, before his talents demanded recognition to lead the Civil Service. But in the meantime according to Chris, he was a jolly good chap and never one to mince his words; his present day record in his years to come, speaks for itself.

The next stop for me, or perhaps it was more of a slow drivepast, was a cruise through the Giriama area before the Mazeras branch-off to Kilifi on the north coast road. It was a much talked about area by the 'culture preachers', who told me to keep my eyes peeled for the beautiful girls on display either side of the road. Accidents were said to be caused by their lack of clothes; their juicy bits and pieces distracted even the most holy amongst us. It was Tharaka all over again, and I shared my senses between them and the road almost up to Mombasa.

I checked into the Rex Hotel opposite the Carlton, just down from the Palace, the oldest and largest hotel in town. Location wise, all three establishments were on Kilindini Road (Moi Avenue) about 300 yards from the junction of the old

Salim Road (Kenyatta Avenue) and the town centre. The Nyali Pontoon Bridge was built in 1931, a year before completion of the famous Sydney Harbour Bridge. It pointed to the north coast and Lamu, and in the opposite direction the Likoni ferry carried pasengers south towards the mysteries of Tanganyika. Of interest to some, the Nyali pontoon bridge was the only one of its type in Africa, but it blocked the sea inlet near to where the Tamarind Restaurant is today. So it was eventually replaced by the new Nyali Bridge in 1980 to open up the creek to larger sea-faring vessels. If you care to look below the Tamarind Restaurant after a tasty meal, you'll see a single pontoon from 1931, a relic from the bridge with a fascinating past.

The famous Elephant Tusks symbolising Mombasa Town were originally built and erected to mark the visit of Princess Margaret to Mombasa in 1956, and they still looked as good as new when I passed under them in '57 on my way to Kilindini Harbour. A port that reflected a happy mood with the entrance open to the public; hawkers gathered at the gates and sold madafu (coconut water) at 10 cts a time to the locals, after which they would sit in a line enjoying the drink with their legs dangling over the harbour sea. Soon after my discovery of this local pastime, I would park my car on the quay and visit the ships if the gang-planks were down. I would take a UK draft-beer and make payment in shillings, the currency used in port. But the drink whilst tasty was usually a lonely affair, with the crew on shore enjoying the likes of the Casablanca, and Star Bar next to the Elephant Tusks. The freedom that prevailed in the Mombasa docks was unbelievable, but if people were enjoying themselves by the waterside of an evening an early demise to their happiness was just a matter of time. And true to form, a couple of years later, the docks were cleared of the public and the gates were locked, leaving only those old enough to savour memories of happier times in the past.

A bare outcrop of rock overlooking the harbour entrance filled my rear-view mirror as I boarded the Likoni ferry with Lunga Lunga in mind; the Kenya boundary was but 71 miles away. Eventually, the Oceanic Hotel would stand tall on that empty outcrop of rock; but for the present the talent to develop that dream was pie in the sky and I had an appointment to keep in Zanzibar Town. My Ford Consul would continue to be my trusty steed until I switched to a plane in the 'haven of peace' Dar es Salaam. A 10-minute hop to my paradise island was all but in the bag.

The map was consulted and the extreme coast road through the coconut plantations in sight of the sea was chosen; not too sensible on reflection, but the shortest route by far. On reaching the boundary I came inland at Lunga Lunga, to sign the book and enter the car registration before I passed into Tanganyika. To my knowledge, Hora Hora on the Tanganyika side of the border had yet to be declared the Tanzanian border town. My arrival in Tanga was heralded soon enough, by the iron bridge crossing and the noisy Bat Caves on my left; Amboni Sisal Estates was straight ahead. These very same estates would be further developed by George Hess and Christina his wife many years later with eco-tourism in mind. George and I first met in the 1980s when we were pounding the streets of Dar looking for business; profitable recollections spring to mind.

From Mombasa to Dar es Salaam along the coastline was too difficult a journey to be enjoyable, toil and sweat was my company, to keep me busy throughout. But in the end, the magnificence of my whole safari far outweighed any stress; emotion alone stopped my car on the Moshi road to pay homage to the snows of Kilimanjaro. I was hooked for life after that, but for the present no more dreaming, we're on the road to Dar.

Despite the passage of years and its recent destruction, I see the double storied 'Planters Hotel' in Tanga Town as though it were only yesterday. (See photo, with a Peugeot 203 in foreground) Ceilings twenty feet high, wafting fans and dinner tables set in Greek style with the plates upside-down to keep them clean until the guests arrived. It was truly a Greek establishment, and perhaps one of the largest in Tanga when it was originally built. Before dinner that evening I made my way into the cavernous bar on the left of the main entrance; in fact it was so cavernous it occupied half the front of the building and the dining-room took up the other half on the right-hand side. These two huge rooms more or less filled the whole ground floor with a spacious front entrance and a central stairway to the verandah rooms upstairs.

Strange things happen in strange places, and let me assure you Tanga was indeed a strange place. A mysterious odour assaulted my senses as I entered the bar and it could only be likened to the smell of old socks worn for a matter of weeks; it brought back boarding school memories, once sniffed, with you for life. It was definitely a socks-like smell and only one person was sitting in the shadows. When you're travelling in a strange country and find a single person in a bar, whether he be a European like yourself, or a fellow African like another fellow African, you do not sit in solitude to fish an occasional fly out of your beer in silence when conversation is there for the making. That's just my own experience; I also accept that other people will do other things. For instance, you don't always get a fly in your beer; it could well be something with longer legs and easier to catch, but the size of the insect is not for you to choose, but the conversation is; it's your karma like the company you keep.

"And what brings you to Tanga?" I pulled back a chair, and the guy smiles as though he knows something I don't.

"A Mowlem tug boat," he replies. Now I know he's English.

"And you?" he asks.

"I'm on my way to Dar es Salaam by road; so far I've driven from the Mount Kenya region to Mombasa and now I'm here for the night." A pride of my achievement was reflected in my voice.

"You poor bugger," he crushed any aspirations I had with just three words. He scratches his head and pulls his beard, his teeth are even and his eyes are vacant, he smells strongly as though he needs a good bath. Perhaps I was a poor bugger who's yet to learn his lesson, but as far as I was concerned my lesson so far was well worthwhile. Adventure was the name of my game and I liked it.

"Mowlem's a household name, an international construction company, so why would it want a boat?" the conversation begins to settle down as I put the question. "Harbour work in Mombasa, Zanzibar, and Tanga, so I rotate between three places as and when my services are required. I'm the Captain and I have a crew of six," he declares the hierarchy.

By now the conversation is becoming interesting and I ask him if he is eating at 'Planters', to which he replies he has a cook on the boat and makes it clear I'm not invited. By then I'm thinking it's just as well, there's a strange smell about him and its getting me down, and the quantity of beer we're drinking wasn't making it any less strong, the smell, not the beer. He had already declared he couldn't detect anything when I asked him what the smell was, so I offered to buy him a beer on the verandah to lure him outside for my own preservation. I desperately needed a whiff of fresh air and I'm already outside with him about to follow, but he raises his hand to forestall any movement as he pulls on his boots to snuff out the smell from his socks; at last his secret is out and the perfume of the night prevails.

"Don't you find it difficult to manage without a first Mate?" I enquired, much relieved by a breath of fresh air. "As I told you, I have a crew of 6 and I have devised a method of personnel management to handle them if they misbehave. They're well paid; I have recruited 2 from Tanga, 2 from Mombasa and 2 from Zanzibar, and I'm sure you understand, I can only beat them when they're not in their homeport. So I 'teach' the Mombasa men in Tanga, and the Zanzibar men get a lesson in Mombasa, that's how it works; you follow?" he laughs and restates his thinking.

"In the home port discipline is bad news for me, so I avoid any confrontation when on home ground."

"Clever, very clever," I had to agree, praising him at the same time. The conversation was moving and there was nothing I could do to influence him one way or another, so I let him continue and signalled to the barman for a second beer to lubricate his tongue still further; he was an interesting character, an unusual man, and I wanted to hear his full story. It was a new angle for me entirely, different and entertaining.

"You asked about a first Mate? Well I did have one for a short while before he jumped over board," he offered a wry smile.

"Why would he jump over board?" I asked.

"Well… he didn't actually jump over board of his own

accord, I personally helped him to get airborne when I caught him sleeping on his watch... hear this?" he pointed his index finger at me to drive his point home.

"We had strayed into the tanker shipping lanes and the safety of my whole crew was threatened by his lack of duty. Then something snapped in me and I couldn't control my temper; he was asleep and a tanker was bearing down on us. Of course, I was sorry about it in the morning when we were one short and everyone knew what had happened, but none said a word about the missing man and neither did I. See this; I wear it to ward off his ghost and evil spirits," he had pulled out a string tied about his neck, to show me a lump of 'nothing' that I could deduce on the end.

"You know these people believe in witchcraft, and as I'm in this area I need protection. This is my charm to ward off the evil spirits." His story continued to intrigue.

"What is it?" I asked, and once more he showed me the lump on the piece of string and held it up to the light for me to get a better look. "It's the leg of a Gecko, guaranteed by my Bagamoyo witch-doctor to ward off evil spirits; especially those of the man who took off for a 'swim' in the middle of the night," he began to appreciate his own rhetoric.

I never did get the name of that English tugboat captain, neither did I ask the name of his boat; whether his story was fact or fiction who knows? It will always remain a mystery to me and to dwell on the truth or otherwise, is a pain best left to posterity. After dinner that night, I took a shower in the company of a gecko high up on the ceiling, his beady eyes were following my every movement, a thought even crossed my mind to coax it down for a bit of protection, much like the man with the 'powerful' socks.

Tanga embraces a unique history all of its own; its clock tower overlooks the harbour and stands sentinel to a cemetery with an equal number of British and German war graves from World War 1, 1914-1918; enemies lie in peace side by side and only their names divide them in history. On this my first visit, my schedule was too tight to understand the tragedy of the befallen, but when the distant future beckons I shall return and my early morning jogging sessions will allow me to read the headstones that tell the story of the forgotten few now sleeping in this hallowed ground. A shower at the new Mkonge Hotel when it is built, is also in the future, followed by a visit to the yet to be established Tanga Cement, where my business lay with my Danish engineering friend John Carlson, with Lisa his beautiful wife, yet to become future family friends. The year is 1980, and a gentleman from England, David Sutton, is the General Manager.

Next morning, I crossed the creek south of Tanga using the Pangani chain ferry; a single car operation. Once the car is on board, the ancient drum is cranked by hand to propel the craft to the opposite side of the creek. The chain attached to the bank behind visually slackens as the drum is manually turned to tighten the chain at the front, designed to draw the ferry across the creek. It was a simple engineering method that had been around for years. It was virtually 'bullet proof' against the wrecking skills of those who worked the to-and-fro action. Once on terra firma I struck out for Bagamoyo, (sad heart) a slave trading settlement with a history of unbelievable misery. A huge 'hanging tree' was still on the shore line in Bagamoyo to bring back memories of the German rulers, who were inclined to hang petty criminals for a present day misdemeanour; a gruesome red rag was flying from the 'hanging branch' when I passed. Bagamoyo was aptly named, and to reach 'sad-heart' I'd struggled across many a shallow river estuary, which only the young and inexperienced would have brazened out. I could have lost the car completely had the tidal backwashes in the estuaries been any deeper. I was both lucky and foolish when I picked my tracks in the watery sand, but with God on my side I'm here to tell the tale.

From Bagamoyo, it was but 20 miles to the capital city to catch the DC 3 of East African Airways to the isles. A return flight of 10 minutes duration cost the princely sum of Shs.53, and to park a car in front of the airport building in Dar es Salaam was free of charge. Apparently, thieves were under control and in short supply; I was assured the car would still be there when I got back.

11

The Zanzibar Hotel was in the centre town; it was built of uneven white-coral blocks many years in the past. A traditional Arab brass bolt and hasp secured the main front door, and I liked to think however unlikely, its brass had been freshly polished to salute my arrival. And what in particular had caught my eye, was the old flintlock rifle barrels used to bar the outside windows. Oddly shaped and embedded directly into the cement without the usual timber frames, they called out to all who used the main entrance, 'look at us we're special.' I'd also spotted a couple of rickshaws parked in the alleyway with their handles pointing towards the sky. These were in 'live form' for me to touch, for the very first time in my life. I would certainly take a ride during my stay, if only to live on the edge more dangerously than before.

On touching down in Zanzibar I was met by John Cumber's brother-in-law, the island's Chief Secretary. He had kindly booked me into the Zanzibar Hotel, the facade of which I've just described. By now I had been on the main island for a couple of hours and was beginning to discover why paradise islands describes them so well. Office hours were 7 am to 1 pm, and the rest of the day was yours to enjoy. Cricket on the 'village green' of an afternoon within sight of the sea was not an uncommon activity. Everyone knew everyone, and unlike the mainland the island was duty-free. A visit to the local museum was a must, if you wanted to learn more about the gruesome Arab slave trade. And before you entered the museum building you are obliged to pass under the branches of a gigantic tree with powerful roots. Said to be over 100 years old, it had witnessed many a slave auction in the shade of its outstretched branches. Livingston's house was an explorer's dream; next door to the sultan's palace on the harbour front, it was almost as big. Finally, I took a stroll in Stone Town and bought a few trinkets; Victorian wall tiles, 999-barrel padlocks, Arab door-bolts and hasps, all of which I have to this day. They continue to remind me of a rich African history, when I was young years ago.

Memories of my paradise island were instilled in me as I collected my car at the airport and headed towards Oyster Bay Hotel; a lazy establishment with palm-clad scenery reaching to the sand and sea. Of an evening, the first floor dining area offered a spectacle of sparkling lights from fishing boats out in the bay, enhanced by a rising moon on a placid sea. By then, I knew it was in my blood to return to Dar many times over, the atmosphere of Oyster Bay was coursing through my veins. Tanganyika, Tanzania, was always good to me; a lovely people in a lovely land sums up the package entirely. An early morning swim inspired by a watery sun rising out of the same placid sea of the night before gave me the appetite I deserved; a breakfast of bacon and eggs in addition to a fillet of fish caught only that morning… Knife and fork together, a last sip of coffee, my safari beckoned.

On the edge of town I pointed the car in a westerly direction towards Morogoro, a perfect day awaited my pleasure. The Morogoro Hotel, but a hundred miles into the interior, could best be described as an ancient monument frozen in time. It had to be haunted by ghosts from the 1920s cunningly hidden in the overhead beams. At the far end of the dining room an ancient theatre stage reminisced of New Year celebrations, loud Charlston music and antics at midnight. Imagine, the Iringa Greek tobacco farmers are in festive mood; the boisterous dancing and the smashing of plates lifts decibels to new highs. I close my eyes and live for the moment as one with them. I'm guiding you, imaginations run wild. What a celebration that was; we enjoyed the moment, lived and rejoiced, another year is born. I'm now exhausted with heavy thoughts and out of breath.

At that very moment, I truly wanted the haunted rafters to sing to me of bygone days and echo the sounds of merriment from long ago; but alas, no sound was there to lighten my lonely breakfast. A scratching knife and fork on an empty plate was the only duet in town. The floor of this incredible ballroom now accommodates dining tables, though in the past it was specially built using timber planks on wooden joists to relax the dancing steps; like those I took as I waltzed away, I had a bill to pay.

Head north to Korogwe, bear west towards Mount Kilimanjaro and you'll reach Moshi town before nightfall; the home of the Wachaga Tribe, the Kikuyu of Tanganyika; equally clever in business and perhaps slightly more refined. Hermann Sarawat, Chairman of the East African Community, was a Chaga and a gentleman, who originally introduced me to Ayub Chamshama of Tanzania Tea Blenders, Sanduku la

Posta 747, Dar es Salaam in 1969, and unchanged today. A mutual business that was to thrive over the years.

On reaching Moshi from Morogoro that morning I squeeze an extra ounce of energy in the direction of the famous Mount Meru Game Sanctuary owned by Dr Von Nagy, a Hungarian national who became my friend in future years, sufficiently so, to show me the very boots he wore when he climbed the mountains to escape the communists in the 1950s. Bundy, his adopted son, did the hard work at the sanctuary and the delightful Birgit was always there to lend a hand. Years later, after the border closure in 1976, Bundy was the friend who ferried me between the Sanctuary and Kilimanjaro Airport, where I boarded an Air Tanzania 737 to conduct my business in Dar es Salaam.

As I have mentioned before and can repeat again and again, this expedition cast a permanent spell of Kilimanjaro upon my soul. To keep my eyes on the road when its beauty overwhelmed, demanded nerves of steel not to stop for another picture. Longido the border post was marked by a small stone sentry box, a well-worn book for the traveller's signature, no passport was required. It was many miles inside Tanganyika, and the box is exactly the same today with a police post in the background. But the actual border is now relocated to Namanga; a place where the Maasai land division was demarcated by the Germans and British; the villains of the plot with divide and rule supposedly fixed in their minds. But with independence such wrongs of the past can be changed if the will is there to re-unite the Maasai tribal lands. Unfortunately, there is a stubbornness in the air and neither country wants to give an inch, so the problem will always be there. Sadly, a Migingo Island situation between Uganda and Kenya in Lake Victoria, yet to be identified as a colonial plot, has similar leanings with no solution in sight.

After passing through the Namanga River Hotel at the border, Kajiado is the next built-up area before Nairobi. The hard rough road, dried up riverbeds and heavy slab-rocks was all that stood between me and a peaceful night's sleep in town. The belching smoke from the brand new cement factory in Athi River is on the horizon and I'm almost home, the capital city and civilisation is just over the hill. A life-changing safari to the tips of my fingers is drawing to a close.

That night I checked into the Grosvenor Hotel, and enjoyed the ambience of the garden with no hassle or doubt about the next stage of the journey hanging over my head; the type of thoughts that keep you buzzing when on safari. A cold beer in hand, what more could I ask? Little did I know it then, but years later, this same hotel would eventually be owned by Peter Gachathi the Permanent Secretary, who would be introduced to me by my future boss Peter Shiyukah. Gachathi and Arthur Mungai the auditor were to become partner-owners of this new Grosvenor venture, where they were seen to be relaxing from time to time in their own garden bar of an evening. I subsequently heard that Arthur had passed away when he was given the wrong blood group on admission to hospital, a tragedy beyond belief. His sister Sarah Mungai of B.O.A.C., close friend to Rosemary Nyagothie of E.A.A., subsequently married John Thiani of journalistic fame. I took the pictures at their wedding as my gift to the couple. One highlight that I recall, was of a prominent guest, Dr. Njoroge Mungai, who delighted the crowd when he heaved a wardrobe single handedly into the wedding gift-circle. Today, the Grosvenor with the restful beer garden is in the hands of the military, but some of the original buildings that overlook Lenana Road continue to invoke sweet memories as I slow down for the bumps near the Russian Embassy. Next stop Meru, 180 miles to go...

The dispatch of my household chattels from Meru to Machakos was already 'written in the stars' and had actually happened by the time I landed at Embakasi after my leave. It was then a matter of 35 miles down the Mombasa road to the 'Machakos Arms' where a banda-room was pre-booked. I was to replace Len Tugnutt the outgoing District Revenue Officer. A man with fingers in many pies describes him well according to Gerry Farrell, who was yet to become a firm friend. First and foremost Len was a showman, and to back up this theory he was driving an enormous Hudson automobile with covered-in wheels, somewhat flashy, a missile in disguise.

12

Princess Margaret, sister to the Queen of England, visited Mombasa in 1956 and to mark the occasion the Elephant Tusks were erected in her honour. The prospect of her presence in Machakos District, had also led to a 10-mile stretch of tarmac from the town to the Mombasa road junction. Unfortunately, when the road was finished, Margaret gave Machakos the slip and missed the view from the Iveti Hills, but left a new road to honour a visit that was never kept. The construction company involved in this venture also built the Machakos Arms, a collection of rondavals where their South African workers stayed whilst making the road; the same place to where I was headed when I landed at Embakasi airport. The Cementation Company from South Africa, had used their soil-stabilisation method to churn cement and soil to form a solid foundation; in its day a revolutionary idea, although some sixty years later the Chinese have perhaps reinvented the same sufficiently well to call it new.

I was told and I listened, because I wasn't there at the time of this revolutionary road and Princess Margaret's no-show, but Len Tugnut was, and as the organiser of this subsequent event, he was assisted by Gerry Farrell. The fireworks bought with Government funds to welcome the Princess were still lying in the stores; Len had an idea, Len had the key, so he was in charge. The idea was to recoup the cost of the fireworks by collecting cash for a display in the area of the Machakos Sports Club. Unofficial ticket books were used to collect the cash from individuals, after which an official receipt was to be issued to re-credit the fireworks costs; that was the plan precisely. The drinking started around 6 o'clock and as the sun went down the crowd increased. In fact, the setting of the sun that evening was the only arrangement that went according to plan, it was in the 'hands of the Gods' and the organisers had nothing to do with it! It also transpired that, the number of 'cooks' to collect the money from the spectators, were far too many to account for the 'broth'.

Apparently, things got off to a good start; the sticks holding the rockets were firmly planted in the ground and all that remained was the means of ignition. What the connection was between a revenue officer, a box of matches and a bunch of fireworks, the spectators were about to find out. The first few rockets shot into the air to come down safely on No. 1 fairway. It was an orderly display at first proceeding in an orderly manner, but according to Gerry, it was unusual for anything to proceed in an orderly manner with Len at the helm. So I suppose, I shouldn't have been surprised to hear that all hell broke lose a few minutes later, when one of the rockets fizzled out and dropped into the fireworks box. The display then changed from the vertical to the horizontal and spectators took off to save their skins; the posh sipping drinks in the clubhouse cringed behind the verandah wall. To end the evening, the final nail in the coffin to bury the whole affair then came home to roost; the cash box had disappeared in the mêlée!

I was subsequently told that the show promoted by my

predecessor lacked organising ability, and the spectators who were mostly Boma staff were banking on the new fellow, that was me, not to be of similar ilk. I gleaned this news in a face-toface discussion with the teller of this tale, soon after my arrival in the district. Whilst I was amused, it also gave me an entrée into Machakos life with a certain amount of expectation from the existing residents. It was the latter half of '59 and by then I'd settled down to a life in the 'Machakos Arms'. As the revenue guy I was obliged to supervise the accounts, for which I was paid a stipend of Shs. 150 per month. A Boma wife looked after the cook and staff and bought the food for the residents, for which she received Shs.300 per month. The Machakos Arms was a well-oiled organisation; the speciality of the house was wild strawberries and cream if you arrived on time. Alfred Vienna, as a pillar of the establishment, knew all about these succulent strawberries; question him if you doubt my word, he's still in town.

The DC's office building in Machakos was of similar design to that of Nyeri; an open square with a white flagpole centred on a grass patch, a main road on the open side. The flag raising ceremony was as important back then as it is today; a dawn and dusk affair. As the 'last post' is sounded at sunset, the flag is lowered and folded in readiness for the 'reveille' call at 6 am the following morning. Tradition has it that the sun will never set on the flag of the British Empire, and neither will it ever set on the flag of Kenya. But in these stringent times we are subjected to the sounds of a puny tin whistle in place of the once mighty bugle, otherwise the colonial tradition continues.

On the left side of the administrative buildings facing the square is the DC's office complete with the fearsome Tom Watts, a big man with a bark worse than his bite; he would growl on occasion from a square-set jaw, mop of fair hair and challenging eyes; according to Molly his wife, he played a fearsome game of squash. As owner of a large American Chevrolet salon his perk as DC was a shilling a mile on government business, despite official transport reserved for his use. It seems laughable in this present day and age when the sky is the limit for claims on duty, but back then I countersigned his unnecessary expense for a shilling a mile with a sword hanging over my head. In the windup to independence, Tom Watts became the National African Courts Officer, and people who knew him in that post told of his mellowing before he finally retired. The second impediment in the Machakos set-up was the human 'metal detector' Bill Ewing the DO1, if you wanted to get a whiff of the DC's hallowed door. And in addition to watching the DC's door in bulldog fashion, Bill also played the part of a happy-go-lucky bachelor from down-under; in the end he tied the knot with one of the girls from the Teacher Training College, much to the delight of Machakos Boma. Great merriment was expressed on his special day, and the last news heard was that of a family man enjoying the antipodean life in the land of his birth, New Zealand.

The DC's wife, Molly, was best described as a soft-natured matronly blond, though few if any in the Boma ever got to know her well. They were not Club people and neither was Bill Ewing. To play games might have brought them too close to us and their authority might have been challenged, but no one had the answer to that, and never was it put to the test. Also housed in the same wing of the district HQ was the District Officer Machakos town; a laid back serious guy who took all the flack from the local villagers in his stride, and none was better qualified to do so than John

Malinda, born and bred in Ukambani. John knew all the tricks of the locals being one of them himself; he always stopped them short before unimaginable proportions were reached. In fact, the whole Malinda family was close knit and an entity of their own. John was in the civil service and Tom his brother was the commercial entrepreneur with a hand in the launch of "Akamba Bus Services." The vision of business magnate Sherali Nathoo, who had established this milestone in Ukambani history. At the launch, the fleet drive-past was spectacular and Tom Watts the DC was present to pay homage. 'Akamba' celebrated its jubilee not so long ago, and even though they are struggling to survive I wish them luck for their centenary in some form or other, years from now.

It was much apparent that Independence was steadily advancing from the first time I set foot in Eastleigh in '55, and my second election experience in Ukambani in '61 heralded a further leap forward; the colonialists were clearly on the way out and the noise from the Mount Kenya region was getting louder! But in the meantime, businesses like Akamba Bus Services thrived on ingenuity. Within a few yards of the town clock stood the biggest shop around. M.D. PURI was displayed on the board and the owner was a super dynamic man by the name of Jan Mohamed. Much admired by Jomo, he held the position of Assistant Minister of Commerce in the first Kenya Cabinet; fluent in Luo and Kikuyu, he was a man of many talents. And in my humble opinion he was the owner of the most beautiful car in town; he also played a professional hand of Bridge, which I knew to my cost. Jan employed two of the most beautiful girls to serve behind the counter in his shop, Amina and Zarina were his stars. As a result, many an admirer would pass by to feast their eyes and perhaps buy nothing. At that time their brother Mahedi was still at school and knew not of his future with Zeenat, the girl he was to marry many years hence. And as this tale unfolds another beauty from that union appears on the scene; her name is Soraiya, and she didn't last that long before Aleem from Burundi took her hand in marriage; they now have a couple of exciting young boys.

Today, Soraiya and Aleem run the Brew Bistro, with 'craft beers' as their speciality. They operate on the Ngong Road and a mammoth extension has recently opened in Westlands; in either place Kifabock brew is king at 6.5%, deep nut brown in colour and my choice on a regular basis; a couple days in the week sums it up completely. On the ground floor of the same Ngong enterprise is a wine shop promoted by Soraiya's Dad, once that little boy in shorts in those far off days. Mahedi now imports wine with his big sister Amina, the glamour girl from the counters of M.D. PURI from years gone by, and his son Khalil, brother to Soraiya, is the modern day whiz-kid with IT to make the business bounce.

Let me call Jan Mohamed, Jan; to match the swishness of his limousine compared to the other two American cars on the block, the Hudson of Len Tugnut and Chevrolet of Tom Watts. Jan's Ford Fairlane in pale green and cream was an icon of the motoring world, such was its beauty. So I wasn't surprised when its use was offered to His Highness the Aga Khan during one of his fleeting visits to Kenya. Sir Eboo Pirbhai, HH's eyes and ears at that time knew exactly what a princely car was all about. His humble taxi driving days had been his teacher, and that Fairlane model in the '60s was there to match the style of all who slipped in through its doors.

The harsh administrative description for the district was 'Machakos', or for those who cared, the soft flowing word that serves the same purpose is 'U-kam-bani', either one disseminates its purpose. The complete package in whatever guise covers an area of almost 6000 square miles, about the size of Yorkshire, the largest county in England. The extremities roughly stretch from Yatta in the west, to Kikumbulyu below Mac's Inn (Tsavo Inn) on the Mombasa road to the East. And let's not forget to mention some of the more famous locations in the district, Wamunyu with its fantastic carvings and their worldwide export trade is closely followed by Kikumbulyu in the East, which offered the most colourful tribal dancing, enhanced by tribal regalia rarely seen in other parts of Kenya. The Chuka drummers from Meru are also worthy of note.

From my failing memory, I recall 25 sub-locations within 4 divisions controlled by 4 District Officers. One Chief was incharge of a number of Sub-chiefs at Locational level. That was the Administration set up when I arrived in Ukambani in '59, similar to most other districts in the country. One tax clerk per sub-location was the usual, with the object of filling the government coffers in Ukambani before the cash was spent on local beer. The Wakamba enjoyed their drink at weekends, and at the end of the month until the money ran out; so caring drivers like myself kept off the roads at week-ends to preserve their licences. The vault behind my office used 2 keys; not only did it hold the government revenue collections but also the receipts to make those collections legal. Trading Licences, Road Tax, and Liquor Licences were part of my lot in life, you name it and I sold it. Interestingly enough, the Local Councils were not running amok with the present demands in 2017, and no such licence was required to paint your bedroom or build a chicken house, to mention a few of the hastles that grow by the day. And as I write, we are about to be hit by a plastic bag ban, which is for the best and a brilliant idea for a change!

Ukambani had their fair share of future Kenyan dignitaries working in the field, to assist with tax collections and administer law and order. A couple of heavyweights that come to mind are Jeremiah Kiereini and Simeon Nyachae, who were treading water in the final run-up to independence. When I next met Kiereini he was a permanent secretary, Njoroge Mungai the minister of defence was his boss, and the government was about to purchase dozens of Vickers battle tanks supported by the Chief of Staff from Ukambani. The purchase was worth tens of millions of pounds and thought to be a costly project in numbers and money to tell our enemies, 'don't mess with us, we have the power!' The detailed brokerage as usual, was shrouded by the military secrets act, though I witnessed on one occasion a single tank-transporter on the Uhuru Park parade. To my knowledge, Kiereini was a snooker fanatic and visited Nairobi Club on a regular basis, and as a man of consequence with serious intentions, he always carried his custom-made cue.

Some years later, Simeon Nyachae became my boss as the Provincial Commissioner Rift Valley Province. And if I recall correctly, it was around this time that the first traffic lights appeared in the Nakuru main street outside the Post Office. They controlled the traffic flow to the provincial offices in the morning, and were there to remind wananchi of who was who. Fortunately, one night they disappeared for the good of the town and we settled back to normal. Had I believed then that Simeon had reached the pinnacle of his ambitions, I would have been sadly wrong. He was very much on his way to the top when appointed Chief Secretary by President Moi, followed by Minister of Finance 1998-99. The sky for him by then was his limit, and our chance meeting in Machakos years ago had long since been forgotten.

Living in Nakuru, as one of the lesser mortals in '63, was indeed my pleasure, but on the other hand Jack Wolff the PC was struggling to accept Daniel Arap Moi as de-facto his boss; the Majimbo era had arrived. Subsequently, Sam Josiah, the most gregarious gentleman I had ever met, took charge of the Rift and replaced Jack Wolff before Nyachae moved in.

However, as I recall, it was Jack Wolff 'the secretary' who sent me the names to pay allowances to the new Members of the Regional Assembly. Daniel Toroitich arap Moi topped the list, and drew an allowance to match my salary earned by experience over the years. The point was made and duly noted by me; heavy regional responsibilities had their merits and just rewards. As I dwell on Nakuru town, 'Madison Square Garden' comes to mind in the early 60s. Just behind the Odeon Cinema, boxing matches were staged in a full-sized ring that barely fitted into the room. Ray Batchelor, the Provincial Sports Officer and my lifelong friend, was the man behind such events; I would lend a hand when summoned to do so. Around this time the four Moi boys were boxing supporters, but it wasn't their father who brought them to the occasion; it was their mother Lena, sister to Eunice, both of whom hailed from Bomet, Eldama Ravine. Years later, I met one of the Moi boys at the Hotel Intercontinental fashion show organised by Salma my wife. He was by then a man in control of life with his bodyguard in the shadows. It was tough to recall those far-off days in Nakuru.

13

The Machakos Revenue Office in 1959 offered another opportunity to hone my election skills, in addition to my usual licencing activities. This time, the purpose of the election was to increase the African seats in the Legislative Council Assembly and the candidates were many. The rules were virtually the same; to make sure the eligible were checked off in the register and cheating was kept to a minimum. Kilome Division was to be my polling station and the year was 1961. Doubt it not; the whole country was buzzing and the two main parties were going head to head; winner takes all, no quarter asked.

The Kenya African National Union led by Jomo Kenyatta in name only won 19 seats; the Kenya African Democratic Union of Ronald Ngala won 11, and 3 independents took the total to 33 African elected members. The balance of 20 reserved seats plus 12 appointed members then made up the full house of 65 in total. But because Kenyatta was still in restriction KANU refused to govern until he was freed, so it was left to Ngala to accept the position of Chief Minister, or Prime Minister of Kenya. I'm stating these numbers in advance of my activities in Ukambani, since they have been in the general domain for many years prior to this retrospective polling experience.

The usual excitement was building as the elections approached. Kenya custom demanded much noise to make the campaign feel really worthwhile, and I had no reason to believe it would be any different from my Meru days. In the meantime, I was privileged to meet many new personalities, clever and not so clever, but in the end it was the job of the electorate to sort the wheat from the chaff. Hopefully, they would get it right and select more wheat than chaff, but only time would tell.

Henry Muli, George Wilson Mathenge and Kyengo Ndile, were but a few of the more prominent personalities who clamoured to enter political life in February 1961. Unfortunately, the Kapenguria Six with Ngei part thereof, were not yet in circulation, and the dilapidated house in Lodwar where Kenyatta stayed I had yet to visit (see picture). It has been renovated since then and looks much better now, but the picture you see was taken in '65 before it gained national-treasure status. Another gentleman by the name of Simon Kioko springs to mind when I think of Dr Njoroge Mungai's health centre in Konza, but for the moment he has to remain in the wings until his election as a Kanu MP in '66 and '69.

My first occasion to meet Tom Mboya was in Machakos town. He'd sped down from Nairobi in his brand new black Mercedes 220S to address a labour union and make us administrators look like paupers. He was driving himself and I would have done exactly the same, if only to get the feel of that beautiful car. Doubtlessly, he was making a statement as Tom Mboya and his car was lighting the way; he had just returned from charming the American trade unions with his fluency and bonhomie for them to be more than generous with their check-off receipts; he also had a load of free and almost free scholarships in his back pocket, one of which went to President Barrack Obama's Dad.

As it so happened, Mungai was visiting his Konza Health Centre on the same day, so he passed back through Machakos town when he heard Tom was there. At the end of their brief meeting, which was more of 'how are you' than anything else, I was standing next to Njoroge when Mboya sped off for our minds to think as one, we were both dying to own such a car. Tom as a true leader, was one of those people first past the post with lesser mortals running to catch up. Charismatic was only the tip of his iceberg, and I honestly believe jealousy discharged the bullet that killed him in the end. When he was building his house on Convent Drive in Lavington, I was on the scene with Peter Shiyukah and Peter Gachathi. They were also building houses on a much smaller scale, without tunnels from the main house to the gazebo in a garden. For them, finance was tight and to manage a garage attached to the house required much thought, though in the end their projects were finished garage and all. Tom dispensed some words of wisdom at that particular time which I took to heart. He said, "I don't own any land other than plots, because buildings are permanent and I don't have to rely on good weather to produce an income." Those were his comments short and sweet, and I have never forgotten such sound advice; though in the meantime, the scramble for farms by wananchi was hotting up.

Not a happy day for me and not a happy day for Kenya. I was seated at the New Stanley Thorn Tree when the shots rang out in Government Road (Moi Avenue) on that fateful afternoon, 5th July 1969, and the public was plunged into shock. Then 15 days later the world hit a high with Neil Armstrong's 'one small step for mankind' on the moon, as Kenyans continued to mourn their grief. Like so many, I shrank from the noise of those shots that rang out, but they meant nothing to me at the time, though I would have been gutted had I known of the evil behind them. Machakos district in '59 and the early '60s was a catalyst for some of the future rich and famous. Charles Njonjo was the visiting Crown Council on a number of occasions, and our local magistrate Sir John Lockhart, Bt. was a hereditary peer of the realm; as a fuddy-duddy with the best of intentions his presence could be awesome; no passionate judgements from him, compassionate he always was. The Courthouse ran parallel to my offices, and the district armoury was on the other side next to the original stonewall of Fort Machakos. It was much like one of the walls in Gedi Ruins, but not in as good condition. Built by Frederick Jackson of the Imperial East Africa Company in 1889 and enlarged by Captain Lugard in 1890, it was the first post built in the East African interior from where John Ainsworth established law and order over Ukambani. Should you wish to know if that period of history is still intact, take a trip down memory lane. It's but 300 yards from the new hotel.

If I recall correctly, Henry Muli owned a petrol station in the Tala Market area and subsequently Paul Ngei was to own a petrol station opposite, but Paul was not able to stand for parliament in 1961 and Henry was, so in the end Henry defeated Mathenge the opposition, to win the Machakos Constituency. That was in February 1961, when Kenyatta was restricted in Lodwar after his move from Lokitaung; regrettably, he had to wait for a few more months to breath the air of freedom. Now if you'll bear with me, I'll try and recall that isolated place of 'Lokitaung' that I eventually visited in 1965; long after the conclusion of these delaying activities. The desolation in Lokitaung was 100% and the Kapenguria 6 had nowhere to go if they managed to escape; those were the actual words spoken to me by Paul Ngei. Roughly interpreted, Lok-Kitaung means the place of Kitang; so named by the Turkana people who occupied the land of their Luhya ancestors. Who or what the word Kitang actually means I have yet to discover, and perhaps I stand to be corrected on these few remarks I have made so far for you to ponder. In Lodwar, I stayed with DC Rotich on that particular visit, but for the moment let me revert back to Machakos.

The honourable Kyengo Ndile was one of the Mackakos greats whose parliamentary seat was eventually passed on to his son, but in the meantime Kyengo the father, and Kyengo the lawyer, was known to flaunt his mortar board and gown on his campaign trails in Ukambani. Those were the days when budding MPs used public transport or hitched a lift, they had yet to receive the pots of gold at the end of their political rainbows. According to Chris Benson the DO Makueni, he would offer frequent lifts to Kyengo to help him with his campaign. And if he stopped for half an hour, Kyengo would speak to the villagers from a position of learning, using his mortar board and gown to great effect. Unfortunately, Chris the DO, and Chris the volunteer driver to Kyengo Ndile, passed on to 'greener pastures' in 2011. But my luck was in when his ran out; I was in London to say a few words about his life as my friend. Chris was a good man indeed, always there to help the campaigner with a lift in pursuit of a political career. Without Chris, Kyengo's victory might never have been achieved; his parliamentary seat to represent Makueni.

It was February 7th or thereabouts, and no one was thinking a week ahead to Valentine's Day. Love was definitely not in the air, but the national elections were in everyone's mind. The two major parties were about to do battle and history was in the making. To open my polling station on time I over-nighted in Kilome at the house of the District Officer Hugh Galton-Fenzi, the son of a famous father who had delighted the motoring public with his pioneering exploits. See for yourself the globe-like monument near to the General Post Office, Kenyatta Avenue. In the present day, I park my car next to that monument when I collect my mail of a Sunday morning. I am able to confirm it's well nailed down to survive the ravages of time, though I have to admit, these days it harbours some additional junk chained to its railings.

KADU came second; there was no stopping the KANU train that was very much on track and roaring out of the station. Once again the electoral registers in '61 had been very similar in composition to those I'd handled in 1957. Symbols and names on the ballot papers with a single box in which to cast your vote after marking the paper. Enlightening it surely was, I even found out what a *kisululu*' was when I studied the symbols, but as you know the answer to that, I won't dwell upon the subject. My Meru voting privilege had been withdrawn by '61, but by then I'd had enough for a lifetime and my loss of a vote in Machakos wasn't an issue. As long as my polling-booth activities were properly conducted I was happy, though I'm the first to acknowledge that someone is always smarter than I was.

After the '61 elections there was no turning back; the word was out and to cushion the shock, compensation was being debated by the expatriate civil servants. A forty-year-old with 10-years' service was in the best position to 'win the lottery', according to the experts. So where was I going with

8 years service at the age of 29, not very far I venture to add. Compensation was linked to the Africanisation programme, job loss, and how long you were likely to spend before landing another. But the flip side was, the longer you stayed on in government the more pension you were able to commute, and that's what I chose to do. In the final reckoning, I stayed on for a further 6 years after independence, a decision that added greatly to my richness in life; fresh blood was in the driving seat and my ambitions were high when I joined Peter Shiyukah at the Ministry of Lands in '66. His warm friendship extended my horizons and I was poised for greater things to come. But before then, several years had to elapse from the time of elation in the 'Machakos Arms', when we matched our benefits to the word of the day, 'Africanisation'. In actual fact, years were to pass before the jingle of coins would be heard in our pockets, but such thoughts were pleasant as we watched and waited for life to catch up. Machakos in the meantime continued to function with a well-worn trail between the dartboard and the squash court, followed by a beer and dinner at the Arms. I wasn't really into golf and the well-oiled 'browns' were not an attractive package; a 'brown' being a 'green' with a sandy surface stabilised by used motor oil, which was no match for the home of golf; St Andrews, Scotland.

A pursuit requiring less energy was a visit to a Nairobi cinema with one of the Teacher Training College girls, all rather cosy, but not always the perfect evening. On one occasion I was told my interlect fell short of her expectations, and she wasn't that brilliant herself. As an alternative, the local cinema offered a cool 2 hours of cowboy films, much to the delight of the 'terrible' three with their interlect lacking. The local Prison Officer John Tilley, the Police Chief Paddy Garland and I, would sit in the front balcony seats with the whole place to ourselves. I was inclined to associate Paddy Garland with the regular arrest of Paul Ngei, our local politician. Paul was a great marcher and usually he chose the high street, from town to the DC's office without a licence. You had to have a licence then, but attitudes to day have changed with the passage of years. In all of his marching days in Machakos, Ngei never managed to get as far as the DC's office, though he tried on many occasions; it was solely due to the vigilance at the police station on route that cut his journey short. Paddy Garland was never one to miss this trick. Ngei, when marching prior to Independence, usually wore a forage cap, the design of which was copied by Idi Amin and the present day military elite; he could well have been a fashionsetter in his own right. He also wore his own insignia 'PG' for

'Prison Graduate' proudly embroidered on the side of his cap. Cast your mind forward many years and once again Ngei is on the move with a personal loyalty march up Kenyatta Avenue to mollify Mzee, who was not too pleased with his party swapping politics. On this occasion, Ngei wanted to demonstrate his personal loyalty by carrying a rifle in the port position for all to be forgiven; after that he returned to his usual life. The 'Kitchen Cabinet' only was privy to Jomo's view, and no one knew for sure why Ngei led such a charmed life with his mentor's support. Rumour had it that Kenyatta owed him his life after a rumpus in Lokitaung, when he as the strongest of the bunch of six saved Kenyatta from a hot cooking pot! That's how I heard it. I suspect the teller of the tale was smoking pot at the time, but whatever the reason there's no denying Kenyatta's kindness towards Ngei.

Much like me, John Tilley was a speck on the map in

Machakos society and when I bumped into him by chance in Richmond Surrey he was retired, but his drinking days in Machakos had taken their toll. And whilst on the subject of John Tilley and drinking, there is a tale about his activities in Machakos town on one particular night, when he failed to make it home and a police patrol found him lying in a ditch. Wild stories in small places spread like bushfires, so I asked him the very next day what had actually happened earlier that morning. True enough, he confirmed he had been 'reclining' in a ditch next to the clock tower in the centre of town, but claimed it wasn't that late at all according to the clock on the tower.

"You see," he ventured to explain. "I mistook the clock for my watch." He did, however, admit to having looked at the time on the tower from a horizontal position in the ditch, and the 3 am looked very much like a 'quarter to twelve'.

"So you see?" John was making a dubious point. "According to the town clock, it wasn't that late when I fell asleep with the hands on my watch in the same position. It was the length of the hands and not their position that confused me. They pointed to a 'reasonable' hour and that had nothing to do with a tipple or two." Clearly, John had been one of us all lying in the gutter as described by Oscar Wilde. And like most of us, he wasn't one of the some looking at the stars.

"The only mistake I actually made was to fall asleep in a ditch, for the bloody Police to shout the news from the top of Iveti Hills!" That was John's confession and retraction all rolled into one, witnessed by the clock tower and the police patrol. Needless to say, security was tight when John was in charge of the local lock-up; he was good at his job in spite of the liquor. The prison gates were always ajar to impound the felons from the Court House. In addition to that, these crazy colonials were giving out vitamin pills to supplement the inmates' diet; mad as hatters they appeared to be.

14

Leave, glorious leave came around for a second time and my name was down for another car loan. On this occasion I had decided to hire a self-drive in London and pick up the new delivery at Embakasi Airport on return. The future ever changes when you think about it, and everything else will change when you're on your way to Nakuru with the Machakos memories behind you. It neither sooths your feelings nor dries your eyes when you relive the highs and lows of Ukambani. So, sit up, wake up, you're now in the present and the future is about to change your life forever.

The brand new VW 1500 cc saloon was a delight to drive and to fully appreciate the scene you had to imagine the grin on my face as I breathed in the newness of the upholstery. I also gloated about its size compared to the Beetle I'd bought in '59, my last foray into the world of new car ownership. The blue body and white roof embellished with a set of whitewall tyres said it all; Palmer was back in town from the land of the Queen. I felt good and full of the joys of spring as I left the Bell Inn in Naivasha and opened up to half throttle, before crossing the single lane bridge just out of town. I was following a bus at the time and running-in the new car engine; not that the bus was jogging along when the police at the roadblock waved it down. I followed suit, observed from a distance and waited; the bus had stopped on the brow of the hill just before the bend, not ideal for overtaking. The plot then began to thicken as I watched the policeman who seemed to be searching for something at the back of the bus, tyre wear and number plates in particular occupied his mind. But by then the long suffering driver was ahead of my thinking and knew the score exactly; he alighted from the cab with a loaf of bread for any wrongs to change to right. The policeman casually saluted to acknowledge the deal, he was then free to go with me on his tail. Piga mafuta, or perhaps I should say kanyanga mafuta, depending on how you see it, but 'hit the gas' is what he did to make up for lost time. Highway hold-ups, stand and deliver, were known to be the hazards of medieval England; how they had arrived in Kenya under a colonial government is for you to guess? Since that incident on the Nakuru highway the multiplication of 2 loaves and 5 fishes are no longer enough, and 'chocolate', once the bribe of choice, falls short of righting wrongs. Today, hi-tech m-pesa, and smelly fifty bob notes tied to door handles rule the roads; it's evolution so I'm told.

At mile 99 from Nairobi, you enter the dip in the main road and pass under the riveted railway bridge that carries the line from Mombasa to Kasese on the Congolese border. Bear left and left again and the railway station beckons; its restaurant is worthy of a high-class meal for transient passengers and the locals, who pitched up for a Sunday roast. In a class of their own describes the serving procedures at the station; the roast is carved and tendered from a trolley wheeled up to your table, with a flow of vegetable salvers in close support. I'm drooling at the thought of this mouth-watering roast all over again. How 'we suffered' as we delved so 'deeply' into our pockets to pay Shs.6.50, a good price for the privilege of that special Sunday lunch. Heavy silver cutlery and crisp white linen tablecloths struck a chord with the five-star Ritz Hotel in Piccadilly.

Chinese chopsticks and noodles are forecast in 2018, if the money doesn't run out before the narrow-gauge rail gives Nakuru the slip. To deny the 4th largest town in the country a visit, as it wends its way towards Uganda, is logic gone mad, but no-one hears the cries from Nakuru county. The Chinese noodles will replace the Italian pizza boda-boda style; they'll arrive at speed by rail and taste delicious, to soften the shock of the growing debt burden. The only other noteworthy restaurant in addition to the main hotels was the Oyster Grill, situated on the first floor of a 1930s corner building in the high street, Donald Avenue. Its excellence was mainly due to an interest held by Darbar's Supermarket; the evening meal with sombre lighting and soft music was the most discrete in town.

I was looking for a place to stay as I passed under the railway bridge in the early '60s. The best hotel in town was the Stag's Head with the Midland a close second, but the parking at the Stag's lacked security, so I checked into the Midland with hanging gates on sentinel columns set back from the Uganda bypass. My Nakuru entry then changed direction to under the bridge and straight on, no left-turn into Donald Avenue. And had I failed to stop at the Midland on the bypass road I might have reached the "Farmers Hotel" on the Molo escarpment. A place where a handwritten menu on a brown-paper bag describes my lunch, before its sale to the GSU.(General Service Unit)

Nakuru Town played host to three cinemas, a racecourse, a

motor sports track, a golf course and a solitary swimming pool at the Lanet Hotel in the vicinity of the Lanet Barracks, where the military-mutiny of '64 was put down by a British army unit at the request of the newly independent Kenya. A lake full of flamingos was open to the public free of charge, and the 'world ranking' Menengai Crater offered fantastic views after the climb.

There were even empty plots across the road from the Stag's Head Hotel when I first settled in, but after independence they fell into the hands of powerful people who borrowed, built, and installed the lending tenants to repay the loans. Absolute power and all quite legal; the Standard Bank then lost its prominence to the newest building in town.

The Nakuru Revenue Office occupied a full wing on the ground floor of the Provincial Commissioner's building, with the P.C. in person on the opposite side up stairs and out of sight; a relaxing thought for all of us. In fact, Nakuru had one of the grandest administration blocks in the country from which to rule the vast Rift Valley province, 70,000 square miles from Kajiado to Lokitaung. Mount Margaret earth station, subsequently renamed Longonot, had yet to be built, but had it been on site it would have shown huge tracts of desert at either end of the Rift with fertile farming belts in the middle; aptly named the 'White Highlands' after the white farmers, who had made their mark by developing choice agriculture land.

From the Midland Hotel I eventually moved into the so-called Cooper Motors Flats; a staggered row of semi-detached houses near to the Public Works on the last roundabout before leaving town. The new Eveready battery factory in the same area, was also under construction at the time. The lower reaches of the town sported a racecourse that doubled as a racetrack for cars when they occasionally came to life. Cricket was played at the Rift Valley Sports Club and a separate golf club was up on the hill. Finally, football matches were held in the municipal stadium and 'Nakuru All Stars', the local team, was where I held the dubious honour of treasurer. Unfortunately, the uncontrollable gate receipts eventually forced my resignation when I discovered the stadium was usually full, and the cash box was usually empty; things were clearly out of control and to catch the thieves would have been a full time occupation. Finally, the last of the three Nakuru cinemas on the way to the racetrack (see photo) was close to Nakuru Tanners and their prestigious lamb's wool slippers offered at Shs.20 a pair. Unlucky for you; I suspect by now, they're out of stock!

I took over the Nakuru office from a methodical man with two feet firmly on the ground. Jack Routledge was about to proceed on long leave with his dear wife Ivy and their three young children, Norman, Allison and Sharon. In the years to come the Routledges became lifelong friends from the very first time we met, but for the present home leave was upper most in their minds. A few months then elapsed before they returned to Nakuru with a brand new VW station wagon as part of their baggage, blue body and white roof, similar colours to mine. Obviously, people with taste.

Nakuru office routine was standard for the course with an increased volume compared to Meru and Machakos, but it was also endowed with a uniqueness all of its own. On the Meru scene, I was expected to conduct driving tests before the ink on my own licence was barely dry from my twice failed episode in Nyeri. It is just possible my incompetence was discovered soon after I arrived; the procedure was quickly moved to Nanyuki. Though in the meantime I'd passed a few learners using my new found authority; it gave me a lift and confirmed my driving skills had merit. In Nakuru I was pleased to learn a driving tester already existed, and all I had to do was issue a licence against a test conducted by someone else. However, my office was unique in another way; I was expected to issue number plates to mobile contraptions if I thought them roadworthy. On one occasion I actually received a bottle of whisky from a grateful mother when I approved her son's contraption; sadly, I returned the whisky with deep regret.

By today's standards the Nakuru office was somewhat shocking in the 60s. The counter clerks were smoking and sipping tea as they served their customers. But for the hi-tech brain of today let me change the description of counter-clerk to 'consultant', in line with the deception personified by Safaricom operators. The 'customer' description also changes to the 'client'. So here's to the consultant and the client and may this elevation of titles not go unnoticed. We're now up to speed with modern day thinking; a spade is no longer a spade, it's a digging implement, bear that in mind. When I was a boy, a dustman in Europe was called a dustman and he tied his trouser legs below the knees with string to keep the dust out; he also wore a flat cap. Today, a dustman is called a 'dust person' for the sake of gender equality, and the bins are on wheels for the ladies, but no ladies want the job. Please forgive me if I digress for a couple of seconds. The final nail in the coffin, or perhaps I should say in the dustbin, is the limitless horizons ahead for those with an interest in garbage. There is now a degree in the subject for anyone seeking high office in Kenya. A degree after all, is a degree, and a garbologist degree must be unique to qualify for a leadership role? For those in the know, this unusual qualification is awarded by the University of Arizona, so why not be unusual and take the course to sniff drains with authority, or perhaps embrace a pungent political career.

Jack Routledge, ex-hurricane-pilot from World War II in the Burma Campaign, was a bit of a smoker much like myself. Though I confined my activities to when I had a beer in hand, no smoking for me in the office; it was therefore stopped forthwith to give our clients a better service. Otherwise, everything else continued as usual with a bunch of settlers ready to beat the 'drum' to Government House if they didn't like what the civil servants were doing. The second string to their bow was their Legislative Council buddies in the reserved seats, still held by the Whites from the time of the '61 elections. They called the tune for the moment, but our time was coming.

Office accommodation in Nakuru was always in tight supply and towards the end of my stay I was shunted to an office in the Ministry of Works, almost out of town and certainly out of sight. The object was to relieve the squeeze in the PC's office building, and to soften this isolation a brand new position of Provincial Internal-Auditor was created for me. It matched my willingness to travel throughout the province and I was likely to be out of the office for long periods of time, which was mutually pleasing for me and those I tended to irk. This new role was a sinecure and as good as a rest and I soon began to enjoy the nomadic life spurned by others. I was my own boss and the quality of my work soon became apparent when the districts demanded my reports in confidential form; some of the inefficiencies laid bare were upsetting those in charge. I have to confess, a hidden smile was usually there from me. The office I had previously shared was finally left entirely to the other delightful young man of my age. Yes, we were young and delightful in those days, although I say it myself, Jagdish M. Patel, or JM was his name. Jagdish knew everything about finance, and my association with him uncovered some unusual aspects in addition to our daily routine. I tried to consult Jagdish on some detail just this last week in 2017, only to hear his telephone answering call, the Kenya National Anthem. His dear lady then sadly told me, he had decided to take leave from his earthly attachments during my visit to UK. I'll miss you dear friend wherever you are?

Praful, brother to Jagdish, was also around when I first met up with Jagdish in Nakuru. He was the Treasurer of the Kericho African District Council on the magnificent salary of 900 bob a month, worth every shilling and a hundred times more. It therefore follows he didn't stay there for very long; he was ambitious and gravitated towards Nairobi to begin his own business in the name of Co-Auto Dealers in Grogan Road, now known as Kirinyaga. Trading is in his blood and no matter how old he is right now, he isn't about to let go; he's in his shop this very morning with boxes on shelves lining the walls behind him. His work is his 'walking stick' in life and he wouldn't have it any other way. I was honoured to attend his 50th wedding anniversary not so long ago, and intrigued by some of his Tanganyika family history from his younger days.

Jagdish stayed on in government after independence and with his wealth of knowledge he was revered by the African nouveau elite, before he moved into the commercial world to fulfil his mission in life. When I last saw him in Nakuru, his office was behind the Odeon Cinema next to the old 'Madison

Square Gardens' boxing arena. Like brother Praful, he had moved into the spare-parts industry on a smaller scale. But before he finally left government, Mzee Kenyatta discovered JM's accounting skills and asked him to be banking his cheques from the Kenya Cooperative Creameries and the Meat Commission, which entailed photocopying the originals for Mzee to examine at leisure, after their banking.

Today, much like his brother, Jagdish could never retire from business, so he resorted to helping his son Sundip at 'Kapu Enterprises' in the industrial area, where he exercised the family flair. But unlike his Dad and his Uncle, who followed the Coronation Safari in '53, Sundip now follows a faster version, Formula One, and pops over to Bahrain from time to time to be in the 21st century.

Rodney Minns from my Meru days (see page 14) and our meeting in the Aga Khan Hospital highlights the talents of Paresh the heart specialist, brother to Sundip; it was my good fortune to meet this charming gentleman for the very first time at the insistence of his father, who wanted him to tend to my illness; for which I thank you Paresh.

Ben Gethi, yet to become a national icon as the Commissioner of Police and Commandant GSU, was the Police Commander in Nakuru when I was there; at that time he had his eye on a beautiful lady called Angela, who was working for Social Services. They dined at my house on Crater Hill shortly before they married, though I don't claim any credit for that eventuality. After a lapse of years, Ben and I were to renew our friendship at the Mayfair Hotel in Nairobi, by then he was running the General Service Unit. He was always affable to me and I enjoyed many an evening with him in the company of

Harun Muturi of ruby mining fame. He used to visit Voi on a regular basis, using his beautiful red Mercedes sports.

Agree with me? Everyone loves a circus and Muturi wanted to bring the whole shebang from India to delight the local crowds; little children would earn him money and were uppermost in his mind. It was a fantastic idea and anticipation was in the air in August '78, thoughts of much pleasure for the kids and much profit for Muturi were almost home and dry by the time the animals embarked in India. That was the plan and nothing was going to go wrong. All the figures had been worked out and the weather was fine, but then the unforeseen had to happen, when His Excellency decided to search for greener pastures and a period of national mourning followed; the Circus was put on hold. Muturi, waited and waited for the ban on entertainment to be lifted, whilst the monkeys munched on big bananas, the elephants tucked into the sugar cane by the acre, and the carnivores kept the meat commission busy. At the end of the chain Muturi was shelling out money and wishing Kenyatta had delayed his departure for at least another 10 days. Following the circus fiasco, our next meeting was at the Mayfair Hotel in September '78. Harun was using a stick to hobble around and it had nothing to do with big bananas, munching sugar cane, or eating meat; apparently, Gethi, who kept a small pistol in a holster strapped to his lower leg had 'accidentally' shot Muturi in the foot; so the story goes. Unconfirmed reports told of Gethi discharging his pistol under the table, much like bladerunner Oscar Pistorius in 2013. Some said it was an accident and some said it wasn't, and many believed the walking stick used by Muturi was only there for sympathy. I actually offered him a chair at my table because of his stick; he then helped himself to spaghetti in the middle of my plate using bare fingers; a messy business indeed, but Muturi was Muturi. The sun was shining and eventually all was forgiven, Muturi abandoned his stick and resumed his usual tipple with Gethi.

Charles Murgor was another gentleman friend whom I first met during my Nakuru days. Sadly, in later years, I had occasion to commiserate with him after a tragic road accident on the railway crossing outside Eldoret, when he lost a family member. Charles was the African Court's Officer Nakuru when I first met him, a similar position Tom Watts occupied on leaving Machakos. He then went on to become the PC Nyanza, ably assisted by his dear wife Christine, whose savvy was as sharp as a needle; and to this day, one of his son's offers legal opinions aired in the local press.

I had no idea why the powers that be would want to post me to Kitale as part of my evolution. For the present, I was merely being delayed at 'the crossing' and as I had just refused Homa Bay I felt obliged to accept this second offer, knowing it was only a matter of time before I returned to Nakuru. This was my thinking when I first arrived in Kitale in '62, suspecting bleak images lay ahead at the top of the Rift. But as the months became many, I was ever grateful to those who had under estimated my worth. True, I had been disappointed at first when I knew not how Kitale was going to change my life. But that was before I hitched my wagon to a 'shooting star', Peter Shiyukah, my comrade in arms.

The immediate area network of DC's in Northern Rift at that time was Joe Musembi in Kapsabet, who later turned up as Managing Director, Express Transport, and Sila Boit in Eldoret, who went on to become Moi's permanent secretary, Ministry of Home Affairs. It was through Sila that I applied for citizenship and swore loyalty to Kenya on a fancy form in special red ink, duly signed and witnessed to the hilt by 'blokes on the bench'. A certain gentleman, who would run the country in the distant future then placed my filled application form in his desk draw, never again to see the light of day. I was told to keep my British Passport; it was more useful for travelling. "If you have a problem about staying here, tell us."

Kitale, metaphorically speaking, was the largest town in the Northern Rift. '64' Eldoret, was actually bigger and carried a farm plot number to add a certain mystique, but for those who lived in Kitale there was no contest, they had the charm that made the town great. The people were diverse, some exciting, some nasty, and there was the usual collection of those who made no decisions and sat on the fence; but whoever they were or whatever they thought, my mind was stretched on a daily basis. When I first arrived, Mike Power was the incumbent DC for maybe a month before Shiyukah turned up to take over the district; by then we both knew it was in our karma to meet. In addition to our administrative duties we became the best of friends, for me to learn unconventional thinking to expand my hitherto narrow mind. A long time ago, it had cost me dear when I failed to conduct a once-in-a-lifetime conversation with Dedan Kimathi.

My exciting sojourn in Kitale, was matched only by a short spell in Baringo for the Independence Elections. Even to this day Baringo still stands tall with exciting tales of tribal regalia, untainted by modern development and evolved over the ages. It blew my mind away to enhance a colourful people; a psychedelic experience beyond belief. (Front cover and inside pictures).

Police airwing Lodwar airstrip; cash office emergency 1963.

Lodwar Boma from DC's office roof, Tribal Police Lines and the white painted DCs house in the middle distance.

With DC Rotich, Lodwar., Tribal Police and mounted propeller from World War ll..

Close up of DC's house Lodwar, where I stayed for 4 weeks.

Kenyatta's house Lodwar, where he was restricted on release from Lokitaung..

Landscape enroute to Lokitaung, where the Kapengiria 6 were free to roam during the day. Alfred Nderi, DO Lokitaung, with hand-built wall by Paul Ngei, behind the sign.

Detention in Lokitaung, showing the 3 rooms occupied by Ngei, Kubai, and Kenyatta. They were locked in at night and free to roam by day.

May 1963, Independence Elections Baringo District; my team south of Akoret.

Stopover in Kapedo; hot sulphur falls north of Lake Baringo; a place of relaxation and a time to eat Egyptian Geese.

RALPH PALMER ─────────────────────

15

As 1963 drew to a close, I returned to Nakuru for a second time with the wilderness of the elections in Baringo still ringing in my ears. What did I leave behind in Kitale when I moved on to Baringo, you may well ask? I claim a revenue office in good shape, though I took away far more than I left behind in the form of memories and generous contacts, my guides to the future. It was the human characters and not the soulless office that gave some heart to Kitale; full of idiosyncrasies with a uniqueness all of its own. Unified by government legislation and divided by individuals, was the opinion of those who stood aloof and observed from afar. The civil servants controlled the town and outside the township was hostile territory in the hands of the settlers. But with the approach of independence, co- operation between the new African settlers and their 'brothers' in the administration was clearly on the cards. The new to-be Prime Minister was almost up and running the country before he became 'Head of State', 12 months later.

On reflection, the Machakos settlers had always been more mature than their Kitale friends, who rushed with their complaints to the Governor's mansion at the first sign of the smallest problem. Complaints in Machakos were handled in a friendlier manner, by a word in someone's ear from Norman Hill, a successful farmer and tennis player, or perhaps from

F.O.B. Wilson, another of the settler greats. They equally used the Sports Club to down a Tusker beer after the sweat of the game, and also in the light of some administrative problem. During my tenure, Norman married a teacher from the training college and had a son of whom he was immensely proud. So much so that, after his birth the Mk10 Jaguar took second place. Now had the civil servants played tennis in Kitale it might have been a more amenable atmosphere, but they didn't play tennis or anything else, so conversation after the game was never put to the test.

The collection of personal tax was through the medium of tax clerks controlled by the Revenue Office in the Town. The top graduated personal tax (GPT) payable for the year was 200/- with no questions asked, unless you wanted to fill in a form and give a good reason why a lesser amount should be paid; ingenuity then came to the fore. The reason penned on one occasion was 'living from hand to mouth', which sufficiently impressed me, to give the benefit of the doubt and enjoy the thought for the rest of the day. Trading, liquor, and vehicle licences were also part of my routine to squeeze the new masafaras, as Sheng describes the suffering wananchi (inhabitants). They were also known as hapless voters, who promoted rogues to pocket the national wealth before their 5 year term runs out. In '62 the district was divided into many social segments and snooker at Endebess Club was playing host to my skills. I would usually take the 10 mile trip to where the tables lay in the company of my challenger, Norman Charlton, Kitale Town Treasurer.

Crampton's Inn, an island all on its own, was a prickly

patch of hostility that went down fighting for the racial divide with a few hard-liners onboard. Crampton the man, in his ignorance, refused point blank to accept any African patrons on his premises, though his hotel held a public licence and he was breaking the law. Unfortunately for me, it was the only place with a pool and that was where I was swimming before I heard of their backward thinking. Even Peter Shiyukah, the District Commissioner in '62, was prevented from visiting Crampton's patch of Kenya. The fellow chopped down a tree to block his way and prevented the police from making an arrest. Eventually, Crampton was charged with a breach of the peace and the liquor licensing board specifically instructed him to open his hotel to all races; he refused and lost his licence. I believe I'm right in saying that his farm was one of the first to be bought out under the Land Resettlement Scheme, designed to transfer white-owned farms to African ownership. On attaining independence, the British government granted tens of millions to look after their 'wayward settlers' with a buy-out programme, organised to meet both sides of the equation; willing seller, willing buyer, financed in part by Britain.

Saboti Location, Kitale District, was a farming area above average in the early 60s, much to the credit of Chief William Wamalwa's administration of the area. It was also around this time that Peter Shiyukah specifically selected a farm in Saboti using his personal knowledge in settlement. Words used by him at the time were, "a long term investment for the whole family in the years to come," which is exactly how it's turned out to be.

Chief William, the person, took a pride in his dress. He was always resplendent in uniform, beset with shining brass buttons and material creases to match his high standards. His Bombay-

Bowler and Kenya Lion insignia was unique from earlier years and commanded the utmost respect, genuinely earned by him. Years later, William entered the Senate and his son Michael, known as Kijana, became Vice President of Kenya. I first met Mick as I knew him, when he came back from America in 1970 bearing degrees aplenty. But it wasn't the degrees that made us one; it was my red sports car that he fell in love with when passing in the area of my future wife's hairdressing salon near to the MacMillan library in Nairobi. The Kenya School of Hairdressing in Avenue House was Salma's business, though at that time we had yet to agree we were made for each other; another year was to elapse before the DC's office took our booking.

Joginder Singh, the rally driver, was the first owner of this white sports car that I changed to red to suit my preference. A Volvo P1800, 1965 no less, with all the good looks and a few of the gizmos demanded by Roger Moore when he played the role of "The Saint" in the first of many spy films, before James Bond, Miss Moneypenny and 'M' gathered fame. The upgraded 125 BHP engine generated a speed in excess of 100mph to transport the latest self-seeking radio, electric overdrive, and let's not forget the driver. That was the position when Mick took a shine to its lines and offered Shs.14,000 to seal the deal. The chrome shield that replaced the Volvo emblem on the bonnet bore my initials and was pledged for return to me after the sale, but I never did get it back (See photo). I met Mick many years later when he was Vice President. He was accompanied by Yvonne his lady whom I then met for the very first time, though she claimed to know me already from the pictures of 'that car' hanging all over her house. "Mick, I see you laughing now and may God bless you both, as I recall our friendship..."

Kitale township had several 'watering holes' of various repute besides the Hotel; one of these was the North End Arms, best described as a popular bar with a local atmosphere and local beauties. It was almost next to the Hill Barrett garage, managed and owned by Jim or Ginger Barrett, who employed a few Whites to dirty their hands as they dispensed their technical skills to the farming community. Hill Barrett was the local Peugeot, Land Rover and Massey Ferguson agent, so its yard in particular, was littered with Ferguson tractors, the farmer's best friend.

Another local establishment with intellectual leanings, aptly describes the Kitale Theatre opposite the Golf Club entrance on the road out of town. When I first arrived on the scene, 'theatrical pun' not intended, it was a semi-functioning theatre sinking under the weight of disinterest, by the new residents of a rapidly expanding town. But to give them their due, a few of the older members were still performing, and prepared to go down with the ship 'Titanic style', should a 'lifeboat' not come to their rescue.

The Sports Club, was in addition to the Golf Club and catered for the younger-set. It was in the area of the DC's house where Peter and Bhila Shiyukah were bringing up the family. Michael, their first born, is now of Kenya Airways fame and a Captain no less. Anne, Daniel and Grace, have also spread their wings and flown the nest from the time I first knew them. The Sports Club was usually patronised by the richer Kenyan Cowboys whose fathers related to the pioneering past; the time when they hitched their cattle wagons to the rails on plot '64' Eldoret, and all that. New Mercedes cars among the youth were not uncommon; the 'Fishtail Merc' with stacked lights was the latest and came with daddy's blessing. My VW beetle was no match for this wealth as a resident of the Kitale Hotel, which was fast becoming a shaky abode even as I stayed there.

When Mike Powers the DC was transferred, his European secretary Julie remained in place when Shiyukah took over as DC. Mahihu was the DO 1. This was a time of changeover in the District Administration throughout the country, which found Peter, Eluid and I, in the unlikely position of sharing a dining room table at the hotel before they moved into their official residences. We all agreed the high ceilings with open rafters echoed the 1920s and portrayed a certain elegance, we also acknowledged a period of transition in Kenya was underway and questioned how long it would take? Sadly, when I returned to Kitale years later the reception area was filled with bags of charcoal, window frames were missing from the guest bedrooms and demolition had started. But I was blessed with happy memories, no matter how ugly the present compared to the past. A particular gentleman I associate with stay at the Kitale Hotel was Charles the headwaiter, who intimidated guests with his immaculate black suit, white shirt, black bow tie and a brilliant smile that lit up the diner's reception. Many years into the future that same dear Charles, the gentleman he always was, turned up at Rift Valley Sports Club. His trademark, a crisp black bow tie was frozen in time, and much to my pleasure he'd remained the same man I'd known from the past.

Now let's get down to some serious business; Peter and Eluid required table etiquette lessons at the Kitale Hotel where our table was set for three. In their frankness, they spelt out their requirements and explained they weren't the types to persevere with local eating customs when advice from me was on hand.

Apparently, their minds were big enough to seek my assistance, though some knowledge demanded of me might well be wanting. The object was to eat in European style to meet world standards, since their new international image was calling and they were not prepared to continue 'African style' and excuse their manners with such remarks as… 'these are our customs and the way we eat at home'. They needed preparation to meet their 'inheritance' and my guidance was sought as we dined at the hotel. In their wisdom they knew they were about to sup with some of the best in the world after Independence, and to excuse their hands-on activities with a village mind set was no longer acceptable; the elite in their new circles demanded better. The handling of posho cake and sukuma wiki (kale) was left entirely upto them, on this subject, they were traditional experts since birth. Whether to be conveyed to their mouths by fork or squeezed in their hand to be squeezed for a second time into their mouths was their business entirely, though this stickiness didn't arise at the Kitale Hotel, or as far as I know, at international banquets. In the present day 2018, prospective ambassadors' take an intensive course embracing diplomatic behaviour that includes wine matching, table manners and general graces expected in high society. Shiyukah and Mahihu in their wisdom were ahead of their time by demanding such training from me, which I was bound to offer with reservation, because I didn't know the lot and told them so. In return they taught me to think outside the box, African style. They told me quite frankly to expand my mind and get rid of my colonial attitude, enjoy life on the upper plane in this new-born era was their advice, by any reckoning. As Mandela would say, *'it's always impossible until it occurs'*, and now the 'impossible' was occurring to me!

***

Personalities like Shiyukah and Mahihu, Luhya and Kikuyu, were typical of the new elite about to become the backbone of the civil service. Racism was out and tribalism was in, and none doubted difficulties lay ahead. Personality, tribe, and whom you knew were your qualifications for greater things to come; university degrees were few and far between. So to combat the lack of qualifications, jobs were awarded in bars with historic names like Wanjohi's, The Corner Bar, The Green Room and Mohinder's to mention but a few, after which an office interview sorted out the paper work. Politics, Tribalism, and then a degree if there was one, were counted in that order. In retrospect, these ancient drinking parlours should be gazetted for the part they played in the history of the civil service. But, as such interviews became less frequent, the Africa Club gifted by His Highness the Aga Khan became the favoured venue.

A hive of activity describes the Africa Club in Jivanjee Gardens after a parliamentary session. The ministers by then had switched to social mood and were debating in a less formal manner about the next day's business. And doubt it not, the who's who in government was there on a regular basis. It was not an unusual sight of an evening to see Mboya, Kiano, Gichuru, Mungai and Njonjo, *propping up the bar*. Some leaned on the furniture, but the elite, Kibaki and Njonjo, usually stood aloof to survey the activities from afar, their tankards smoothing their waistcoats. None of these honourable gentlemen was ever lost for words and many a good story was there for the telling, when the company was right. They were friends in legislation and friends in life, and nothing was going to change their stance. They would drive themselves to the club from parliament without any pomp to emphasise their standing in the community; the size of their ego was not their aim in life. In particular, Tom Mboya would never hesitate to tip a beggar between him, his car and the club, and pistols in brown paper bags would gather dust in car-door pockets. Even the handsome J.M. Kariuki would push into the club from time to time of his own volition. Though not a member, he was far too bumptious for anyone to throw him out. Celebrating New Year's Eve at the Africa Club was the highlight of the year. If you really got lucky you'd be in the company of the government greats for the midnight ceremony before they disappeared, having shaken hands, hugged the many, and wishing all well. In those days the police band would pound-out 'proper' music with a touch of Ghana high-life in vogue at the time; come midnight *Auld Lang Syne* would hit the spot. Call me old fashioned when I think of such tunes, but memories will always be memories, ingrained for life and never forgotten.

On one particular New Year's Eve I was accompanied by Rosemary Nyagothie, niece to James Gichuru, Minister of Finance. Her mother managed things at the Norfolk Hotel and Rosemary was flying with East African Airways. After midnight, as I recall, *Auld Lang Syne* was belted out by the police band and the Conga dance Kenya-style took over. The custom was to hold the waist of the lady in front and form a line behind the leader; the 'me too' movement and the pinching of things your fingers were itching to do, was still under wraps. The Conga snake then gathered pace to the rhythm of *Kanu njenga nchi* played by the band with the chants of the revellers keeping time. As more people joined in the fun the band was left behind in the club, for the chanting of *Kanu Njenga Nchi* to keep the timing and hit the cool night air. A leg out to the left was followed by one out to the right, *njenga nchi* led the way. With perhaps a hundred in line, the snake-like dance reached as far as the Garden Hotel on the corner of Market Street, before returning to the club via the trees in Jivanjee gardens for another beer. Credit for such jubilant evenings goes to the Honorary Secretary Dr Jimmy Nesbit, a medical practitioner, gentlemen, and a person who offered his voluntary services to make the club great.

The government of the day was driven by strong willed people who had themselves in mind; matured over years, they had joined the struggle towards independence. Whether they were inside the civil service or playing a part in the political machine made little difference; the whole nation was on the move. Politicians and civil servants were closing ranks, sparked by ambition. Those already in the 'old boy' network *colonial style* claimed it was working well. Alliance High, under the guidance of Carey-Francis had played its part in bonding personalities, but the degree brigade was somewhat limited and had yet to acquire the honourary doctorates used to impress. The higher learning establishments and the lack of education outside government circles was pushing for the Ndegwa Commission, to allow private business in parallel with government jobs. Such self-serving legislation was designed to legitimize the dubious activities by civil servants since independence; corruption was poised for greater highs and the fallacy of the brain drain that never was, was about to disappear.

The Ndegwa Commission was duly enacted in 1971, to favour private business in office time, which literally put the fox in- charge of the hen house. If it wasn't so sad, these humourous activities spawned by the commission would be the butt of many a joke. Jackets with empty pockets were actually left on the backs of office chairs to show the owners were doing government business, but in actual fact the jacket had been there from the day before for the secretary to dust when she arrived in the morning. Business skills of the civil servant then raced ahead and the quality of the jackets then changed to 'gold', with an up-market label stitched on the sleeve.

To the enquiring mind, can a civil servant or country rep. conduct business without the leverage of the job, refer to the Nation, Star or Standard newspapers. In the early days after Independence rumours were rife, both true and false, about streets of houses exchanged for road contracts and generous military kickbacks were also in vogue. With the passage of time they are now called 'legacies' to disguise the smell from the '60s; now a joke by the new county 'eaters'.

As I moved into the Kitale Hotel, my preferred life style of properly presented food without the hassle of catering became my pleasure once more, though the luxury of the Outspan would always remain a lifetime experience never surpassed. The event of the week at this new establishment was held on a Tuesday and called "Farmers Day." As I found out to my discomfort, it filled the hotel reception with a jostling crowd that pushed me and my curiosity into the shadows. I can hardly say I stood back from the crowd and observed, when the crowd was actually in my face and echoed a past generation frozen in time. In the present it surely was, but it depicted the past and none could imagine the future. A withered face and melancholy eyes embraced the mood, a loathing to leave behind beautiful farms developed over the years. There was a noticeable reluctance by the white farmers to accept the swallowing of their history, at breakneck speed. The peaceful transfer of land on a willing-seller willing-buyer basis was progressing well, but more slowly than expected. However, whatever the pace, the credit for this whole exercise belonged to the Honourable Jomo Kenyatta, who graciously tolerated the errors of the past to favour his country's future.

Of additional interest to me was the Kitale cinema; the architecture was from a period in history when elegance was an important feature. Built in the 1930s, its original debut offered silent movies with 'Charlie Chaplin' as the hero, but since then sound was added to promote cowboy films, popular with the locals, and I had to be included. Worthy of note was the seating layout on the basis of them and us, but where you sat was entirely up to you; the high-rollers would occupy the boxes and the riffraff were down in the front. On occasion, a boring film would encourage noises from the boxes in addition to crispy chip packets, and those in the know blamed the girl from the Kitale Hotel who was usually bored more often than not. Rumour had it that her ankles were sometimes spotted above the balcony parapet, far enough apart to doubt they were joined in the middle. But much to her credit, she was always back in reception before the theatre audience returned to the hotel bar. Though her behaviour was doubted by most, they enjoyed what they heard from others rather than what they saw for themselves. The overall social life in Kitale was not too bad, but the North End Arms seemed to be the only alternative to the hotel if you were not a member of the club. There was also a division between the settlers and us in the government, which they felt was falling apart with a couple of Africans at the helm, Shiyukah and Mahihu, and I the traitor, was the difficult one to place. Neither of the Africans played any known sport and all I could manage was snooker with Charlton at the Endebess

Club, and that didn't count as a sport; the swimming pool at Crampton's Inn had also been abandoned by choice. Though I didn't know it at the time, I was due to restart golf in the 1990s at Kabete Nairobi, with a certain amount of persuasion from Philip Horobin, my friend-to-be in the distant future and a present day editor, with all the bells and whistles concerning this book; Philip, I owe you. Lawn Bowls at Nairobi Club also began to occupy a portion of my life in the 90s, thanks to a friendly invitation from Zippi Miano and Leila, who invited me to join them when they saw me slinking past their gate intent on a dip in the pool. Since then I have progressed but a little and I'm indebted to a couple of current day bowlers, who took the time to comment on this book, somewhat kindly I hasten to add. Mike Karanja the Capitan, and Pio Munyingi the best lead I know; to both I am truly indebted.

Peter and I quickly became the best of buddies for life in the years to come, but at this point in time we needed big town life to stretch ourselves and Kitale was clearly a place in the sticks. So questions were posed and distances gauged between two places where civilisation was bubbling hundreds of miles apart. To be precise, Nairobi was 250 miles and Kampala 200, so Kampala usually prevailed. With no border restrictions and no passports needed we would cross into Uganda at Malaba, to meet a single track of tarmac that stretched as far as Jinga Town.

The ancient 'Rippon Falls' hotel in Jinja was a familiar sight from my first visit in the fifties; I had over-nighted there on my way to Kasese, the Mountains of the Moon, Bundibugeyo, the land of Pygmies. A collection of timber rooms on stilts from earlier colonial times describes it well; it was constructed years before the hydro-electric Owen Falls dam dominated the area. A couple of new hotels were then built enroute, the 'Rock' in Tororo and the 'Crested Crane' in Jinja, to become my new staging posts in place of the Rippon Falls Hotel, where ants with big teeth were chomping the ancient wood timbers. In fact, the Rock Hotel Tororo became my favourite launch pad, either into Uganda, or for a last drink before taking on the Kenya roads. Had it been raining, the mud on the Kenya side would usually dry out by the afternoon, so in the meantime a spectacular view was there for the taking. Once on the Kenya side, Webuye and the Pan African Paper Mills project was but half an hour away. According to some, this mill was one of the first foreign rip- offs absorbed by Kenya with government support. 'Expensive' second-hand machinery from India valued as scrap back home, suddenly gained great value when landed in Mombasa; to represent the Indian share holding in this company. Then, to match the value of the second-hand 'scrap' investment, poor Kenya paid hard cash for working capital and a shareholding; to end in doom in the not too distant future. In the meantime, a ban was placed on superior paper imports at lower prices from overseas, to subsidise the local mill production. Roofing-felt paper imported from Canada for Cassman Brown in the '70s was of my personal interest, but the uniqueness of this exclusive product was not exempted, so standards suffered.

The next stop after Webuye was either Eldoret or Saboti via the home of the Wamalwa's, a Vice President in waiting and son of Chief William, previously mentioned. But as I dwell on the Kenya/Uganda border area, I feel bound to recall my fleeting visit to the recently built hotel in Mbale, where I expected to stay when I attended a wedding at the local Cathedral;

Shiyukah's cousin was getting married. I recall the church was new and very large, so whatever its status, Cathedral describes it well. And whilst in Mbale certain things came home to roost; there was 'no room at the inn', so I had to look for a 'stable', or return to Kitale that very same night. My one and only Mbale adventure then began to unfold in the shape of a banana draped room, or perhaps a banana store describes it better. And as I hadn't slept in a banana store before, it would be a brand new experience. Imagine my surprise, an attractive young lady from the wedding had taken pity on me, to dispel any thought of my immediate return to Kitale; she had invited me to stay over. The shadows dancing on the makuti thatch that night from a flickering candle beside the bed created a memorable moment, but in the end it was the young lady who 'burned' brightest of all.

The Mercedes bug I'd caught from the younger clique at Kitale Sports Club was further encouraged by Peter's new Citroen with super-air suspension (see photo). I badly needed an upgrade and was about to do just that. Nairobi, I'm on my way with a few coins jingling in my pocket. A VW trade-in for a second-hand Merc. was on the cards. Pre-owned sounds so much better you must agree, but whatever the description, the 190 Ponton was the first of many Mercs I fell in love with. So, soon after my arrival in Kitale, (see photo) my VW changed to a Merc, which became our safari transport, as Peter and I took turns at the wheel on our jaunts to Kampala. Red bodied, cream roof and whitewall tyres, bench seat, Becker self-tuning radio and column change were a few of the goodies on offer. The ivory steering wheel with chrome horn-ring was indeed a pleasure to hold; let alone behold.

KENYA MATTERS

Happy days; Peter Shiyukah, PS. Jesse Gachago Asst Minister, and James Maina Director of Settlement..On my Nyali Beach Hotel verandah in the 60s.
Below: El Molo fisherman Lake Rudolf 1964, population about 200 in total.

Austin 3 tons, a rough tough mode of travel when no Landrover was available.
My Merc. over looking the Kerio Valley, used on occasion to give William Ole N'timama and Ruben Chesire a lift to Nakuru from Kabarnet, where we worked as a team.

KENYA MATTERS

An impressive tribal gathering in Lodwar.

A world record-breaking termite/anthill, 20 ft plus, Baringo district 1963.

Baringo 1988, 25 years later with brother John, different termites, same idea.

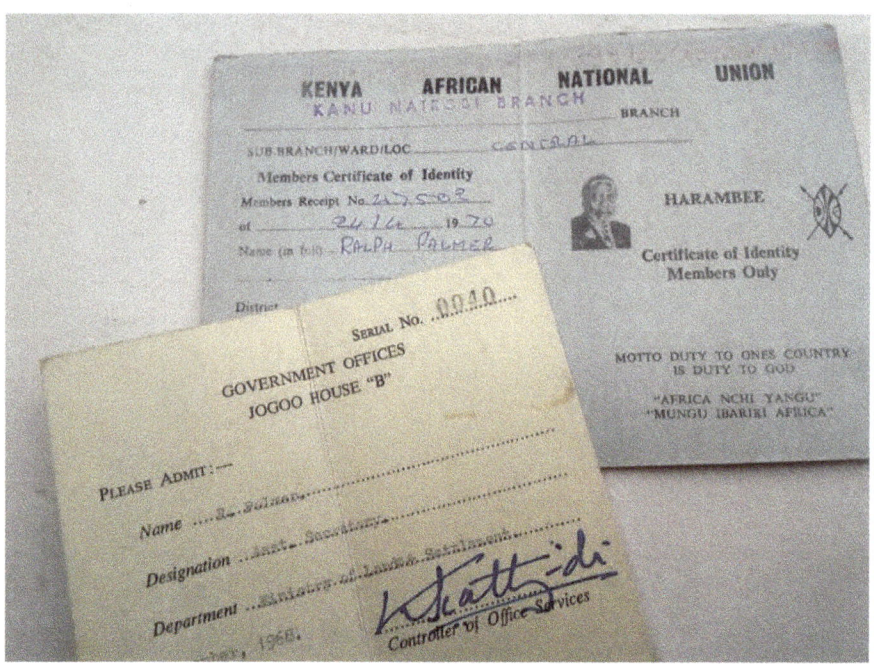

An active member of the community

Nakuru race-track in '61, well before houses took over..

16

Some of the delights I recall in Kampala were centred on the Crystal Springs Hotel, an establishment boasting the largest swimming pool in town. When I stayed there, I would usually lodge in one of their bandas next to the pool if I was on my own, but when I was with Peter I never really knew where I would end up, so I'd usually leave my luggage to hold the room in case I missed a liasion in town. However, if I felt really lucky I'd not book into the Springs and change for the evening at Makerere; a university with some of the narrowest corridors in the world; they should have been mirrored to make them look wider. After which we'd split; Peter had his agenda with his university friends and I had mine with the glamour in town; that's what the journey was all about. But one thing was for sure; we'd fix a meet for the following morning to drive back to Kitale, each in turn taking the wheel as part of the outing. Mobile phones not yet, though Kampala with its seven hills favoured smoke-signals or flashing- mirrors, had you the inclination.

Undoubtedly, Kampala was, and still is, the capital of the 'Pearl of Africa' as Winston Churchill once described this beautiful country. Each hill in town had something to say; the

Cathedral with the saintly bones, the White Mosque with the Scriptures on the walls, and let's not forget Tank Hill designed to pressurise the water system; these are but three of the seven to whet your appetite towards the other four. The Crystal Springs was reached by way of the Port Bell Road, and the Waragi factory noted for its pureness of spirit. Years later, Waragi was followed by Konyagi in Tanzania and finally Kenya woke up to the idea and created Kenya Cane. I still retain a half-bottle of Uganda Waragi collected from Tororo town on one of my jaunts in the 60s. It lodges in my London bar and remains as potent as the day it came off the shelf; an occasional nip is not denied. It cost Shs10 when the power of East African shilling extended to Aden and Somalia.

An ethereal calm before the political storm gave birth to the sweet life in Kampala; the question on every ones lips was how long will the present last? As it so transpired, King Freddie ruled as Frederick Muteso II, Kabaka of Buganda until '69, before the storm clouds burst to reveal the ugly side of life. The kingdoms were trashed overnight and the ruling classes were reduced to ordinary citizens. Obote, the most common of the common man was being nasty; he envied the royals their breeding and they were also better looking. Politics and jealously had finally erupted to remove the thorn in his ego and trash the playground of Africa over night. The famous Royal Mall that led to the Bunge faded to insignificance, and the Katikiro would no longer enact the laws for the most powerful kingdom in the country.

The wait was now on for justice to strike back in the kingdom's favour, but for the present Obote held the reins of power with the help of his foreign trained security. The first chink in his armour appeared when the chopper of Oyite-Ojok of the State Research Bureau suddenly dropped like a stone from the sky; a good omen appreciated by many. God at last was on the side of kingdoms and muted rejoicing was heard behind closed doors to match the tone of events.

A second Kwame Nkrumah is a good analogy for Obote, and much like Nkrumah, his time was running out. Idi Amin was scheming to sack the sacker of the kingdoms, but the Malaysian Conference and Obote's demise was still 2 years away. To digress, Shiyukah and I also shared a strange affinity with Obote, who to his credit liked old buildings similar to the Crystal Springs and the Imperial Hotel in Kampala, richly endowed in history. When he stayed over in Nairobi he always lodged at the Norfolk Hotel, the place with the iron wheeled tractor and rickshaw-buggy that seemed to have come along with the building; they are there to this day as they were back then, check them out should you care to do so. When I stayed at the Norfolk, No. 52, just off the front verandah and next to the terrace bar was my favourite room; old fashioned with a cavernous ceiling describes it well. Unfortunately, it was eventually demolished to make way for development, which is the story of my life when I look back over the years, but whatever my thinking the 'Norfolk' remains a wonderful place.

The night life in Kampala, was well worth the drive from Kitale. The gyrations of the gorgeous girls loosened by Lingala set the senses free and rattle the roots of Africa. Such entertainment changed the scene from cold to gold as the nights wore on and souls floated free, the end of the world could come and move on, it would make no difference to me! The White Nile nightclub, nestled below the hills on the Entebbe airport road. Its main attraction was a multi-arched verandah of Moorish design that embraced the inside activities, though compared to the Top Life their revelry was mediocre.

The real show piece in town and the largest night-club in East Africa, was beyond doubt the Top Life. Unfortunately, when Idi Amin took over the name was changed to an insignificant something or other, for it to lose its magic; dangerous uniformed soldiers, drunk, jealous and armed roamed the dance floor, and you entered at your peril. But whatever the odds, I was blessed to embrace the original club; an old fashioned wood raftered building within sight of the Kabaka's Palace and the Bunge (parliament). It was indeed the area, where the Royals laid claim to hallowed land.

A third establishment of note was a famous restaurant, or perhaps infamous describes it better, so I'll leave its appraisal to you, when you know what it's all about. This downtown enterprise was somewhat fancied by those who knew of its 'secret service', and it had nothing to do with James Bond. The name was Joanna's and they provided cubicles with curtains for privacy during your meal, with food on your plate or a waitress on your lap; a 'sweetie' in human form. The choice was yours in the upstairs rooms at Joanna's, and they came at about the same price, with a largish tip to match the added 'flavours'.

Each of the two main nightclubs employed two bands alternating at 2-hour intervals from 8 pm to 8 am. Their range of music oscillated between Ghana highlife, Congo beat, Lingala and the latest from USA and Europe with no pause for breath. 12 musicians were on stage at any one time, to produce a deep down resonance endemic in their bones from birth. In modern parlance, the joint was roasting out of control and floating free. At the Top Life the dance floor was huge; the wooden stage occupied by the band was on joists to give the rhythm a chance to breath; and on occasion the stage was seen to dance alone urged on by those in attendance. At either corner of the stage a maize- pounding, pole-like-stick was affixed; but these were poles with a difference and very special when put to the test. Their purpose in life was to anchor the lady above the waist, for her buttocks to shake and gyrate to the beat of the supernatural gone wild! I would even get carried away myself, not by gripping the poles but by shouting some nonsense to be in with the crowd, and no one seemed to notice, I was out of tune.

As the night wore on and the small hours of the morning approached thoughts were building; accommodation had to be found and I was looking. True, I had the option of an hotel room, but the visiting custom was usually stretched to sleeping- out to get the feel of other things, if you know what I mean; we were only just in the second half of the twentieth century and killer bugs were under control. The car was always safe wherever it was left and none was anxious on that score, but your choice of a generous good mannered girl with passion and a room for the night had to be balanced against the beer consumed; and it didn't always work out for the better at 3 am in the morning.

On one occasion when I found myself in a strange bed, my partner whispered in my ear, "tuck your toes in under the sheets or the rats might eat them." After which, I was assured that if that happened the eating was quite painless; the rats would first blow on your flesh to anaesthetize the surface before they tucked in to eat you alive! Finally, you fall asleep with the aid of the beer that deadens the scuttling noises on the tin roof, and with luck when you awake in the morning, nothing is missing.

There was also the one room scene, where a string with a

curtain divided the kitchen from the bedroom; it could also serve to keep a bunch of matoke, green bananas, off the floor. To tell who was who in Kampala was a tricky business, when most ladies dressed in high-fashion of an evening, kilemba (head scarves), beautiful bodices with high shouldered sleeves and the tightest of skirts to emphasis their buttocks... a shake of which drove men crazy! Bling, glorious bling, finally filled in the gaps to grab the senses. Sometimes, I struck gold, to find myself in the Kabaka's compound when I awoke in the morning; an honour of the highest esteem. The royal lady then served an English breakfast from a kneeling pose as I sat in an armchair like her 'king', freshly bathed from the tap in her bathroom. A magnificent experience by any measure; cold water, hot food, think about it and drool. I know I will never see such times again, and as for you dear reader, life has sadly passed you by. This was an era when a white man could live off the reputation of those who had gone before, and to add to my pleasure I was surrounded by some of the most beautiful women in the world. It had been my good fortune to have lived as a 'king' for only a few hours, a 'lottery win' to cherish for life.

Those who now live off the administration of poverty and brandish diplomatic passports, back-packers, modern day iPhone zombies, university gaps and voluntourism had yet to impinge upon my sanity. I blessed my mother for timing my birth to coincide with these Uganda ventures. Robots, I.T., A.I. and noisy matatus will arrive soon enough, but for the present I'll rest my head in my hands, breathe in deeply, the African rhythm will sooth my soul.

For revenue control, Kapenguria District with its dark memories of the Kenyatta trials and the famous 6 was under my direction. And Lodwar, almost off the map, was the deepest colour in the spectrum. In retrospect, travel though tough to these distant areas added another exciting dimension to my life, all expenses paid by a grateful government. To reach Lodwar by road in the 60s one had to pass into Uganda at Amudat trading centre south of Moroto, the capital of the region and close to Obote's Acholi origin. The dirt road was overlooked by abandoned concrete block-houses built to contain the Italian threat from Ethiopia in World War II. These historic piles of concrete will always be in place on the old Lodwar road, so pack your bags and get behind the wheel if you want to reflect on history. Such fortifications are more trouble than they're worth to remove; a similar scenario exists in Bremen-Haven Germany with U-Boat pens so vast, they'll be in place when global warming drowns the earth.

Lodwar was at the end of the world, or so it seemed to be when I stayed with District Commissioner Rotich; a more delightful guy you couldn't wish to meet. (See photo outside his office.) Those were the days when we were simple people; no trappings of power with whistles, ribbons and peaked caps; your personality was your rank in the community. Of an evening, on occasion, we would replenish our liquid balances by sinking a case of Tusker, 24 x 1pint bottles between us, before we turned in for the night to lose all the liquids in a sweat-soaked bed by morning. Conscious of our health and rehydration to balance our equilibrium, we would then start all over again with the same routine when the demand was pressing. Believe it or not, we were never 'high' on booze; it was more of a medicinal thing to maintain our hydration, though I don't deny the treatment spoke well for its administration.

Little did I know it then, I was to cast my shadow in Lodwar on many future occasions without a thought for the generous supplies of beer.

The DO Lokitaung, of subsequent Kenyatta Airport fame in the Capital City, was Alfred Nderi. (see picture). His office overlooked the housing, or perhaps I should call it the cell-block where the Kapenguria 6 were detained and obliged to cook for themselves. With no planning from me, Paul Ngei, a Minister in Kenyatta's Government had decided to take a trip down memory lane on the very same day I pitched up in Lokitaung. He kindly explained the area he knew so well from his cell-block days, and in particular he expressed his pride in a rough stonewall he had personally built by hand; it is to the right of Alfred Nderi's office, behind the sign in the photo. Not very impressive as you can see, but I didn't tell him so. He also led me down the hill from the office to point out Kenyatta's empty room next to Fred Kubai's and his own. Achieng Oneko, whom I knew in later years was on the other side of the building. Apparently, the cooking of meals was conducted on the concrete slab immediately outside their doors using an enormous sufuria balancing on a small jiko or stove. Meat stew, rice or posho was the usual; he further declared the sufuria to be big enough to accommodate a small white missionary if found lying around; he laughed and I joined in, not being a small white missionary, and I wasn't lying around. (see picture of building). Whilst the rooms were empty, it was not hard to imagine the past intrigues lurking in the mind of Ngei, when he dared to dream in the past on that particular day. 10 miles north of Lokitaung and you're in the filming world of 'Beau Geste', where a site was surveyed on the shores of Lake Rudolf for an epic Foreign Legion film in the late 1930s. Dramatic scenery and a ruined fort was sought to fit the bill, but with California on their doorstep the Americans picked a spot nearer home. So after much hype about Lokitaung nothing appeared worldwide, but Lokitaung for me was a mind-blowing experience with an indescribable emptiness. (see picture of my vehicle on route) It made me doubt Nderi's job was enough to keep him busy, but only he had the answer to that. I returned to Lodwar that very same evening to recharge the liquid balance in my system and to reminisce with Rotich, about another great day spent surveying history. I cannot recall who it was, but someone once said, 'beer is proof God loves us', and I'd be denying the truth if I didn't acknowledge his love for us in Lodwar.

Senior Chief Ngeleyo and his warriors, waiting to vote.

Moran waiting to vote; front cover insert is moran on the left.

KENYA MATTERS

Top left: Baringo with East Pokot friend. Right: Philimon arap Chelego, with his family. My cook for 3 years, before promotion to the kitchen of Vice President, Danial arap Moi, at Kabarnet Gardens.

1963 President Kenyatta visiting Nakuru in the company of Haile Selassie. Enjoying his white Lincoln Continental, an Independence gift from the American people.

1958 flood, Mackinnon road, on route to Dar es Salaam via Mombasa, 1955 Ford Consul.

Volvo P1800. 1st owner Joginder Singh the flying Sikh, then Ralph Palmer, who sold it on to 'Kijana' Mick Wamalwa, Kenya Vice President in waiting..

KENYA MATTERS

Shiyukah and Palmer on safari '66

50 kgs. Nile perch, Palmer, and Bob McConnall, fisheries officer Lake Rudolf, (Turkana)

Basking crocodiles, waiting for the birds to pick their teeth, Kampi ya Samaki, Lake Baringo '63, election time.

17

The General Elections leading up to Independence placed me in Baringo Revenue Office. I'd just taken over from John Vaz, who was having a difficult time with the famine relief and the floods all rolled into one. Once again, I was asked to help out a married man and by way of thanks I was promised a quick return to a grade 'A' station with more social facilities, something a bachelor so needs. Until then however, I was expected to help with the national elections, perform the humdrum duties of paying salaries, collecting taxes and anything else the government could levy to make a mean buck; much like the 21st century today on a less scathing scale. Kabarnet could best be described as a remote hill station with a small row of government offices, and another small row of residential houses to underline its insignificance.

Historically, Kabarnet District had experienced a dramatic past when drought swept through the area between August 1927 and April 1928, to be compounded by a miserable harvest eaten by swarms of locusts; unfortunately, many deaths were recorded. To save the situation famine relief was dispatched from Eldoret to Tambach by lorry, to be man-handled by over a thousand wapagazi, porters. One sack of posho per head then moved it up to Kabarnet. Marching songs gave pace to dramatic lines that coursed their way across the Kerio valley. The Zanzibaris on safari in the 1890s also mention Baringo in their marching songs. 'Hurry hurry as far as Baringo, and a little bit further we reach Uganda. Upesi upesi, hata Baringo, mbali kidogo tutafika Uganda'.

Fast forward; welcome to Kabarnet in 1963, a place where the Tilley lamp is king when the sun goes down. The nearest trading centre is Kabartonjo, a collection of corrugated iron shops hardly worthy of a trading licence between them. The goats are surprisingly laid back as they forage for empty cement bags to chew, and the hens that cluck and scratch in the dirt were known to let an occasional egg drop for the rats to suck, if a diligent owner didn't catch it first. This is the year of the big vote and the trading centre is abandoned for a political meeting in the chief's office, leaving a bar of soap on one of the shop counters to keep an eye on the street. The nation is in a trance and the inhabitants of Baringo are looking forward to better things to come, but they have seen such hype before and miracles rarely happen.

'Write the remainder of this year off,' a wise old man suggested. 'That's not the way things happen', advised another, wiser, wise old man.

But whatever their pros and cons, they both agreed that the election fever gripping the country is all about the 'power' to steal from the poor, and wishful thinkers were living high on bribes in the run-up to the voting. The two main parties locked in battle were KANU, the Kenya African National Union led by Jomo Kenyatta, and KADU, the Kenya African Democratic Union led by Ronald Ngala. Baringo, a KADU stronghold, was represented by the local boma politico Henry Cheboiwo from

Kabartonjo, who was up against the personage of Daniel arap Moi from Eldama Ravine, both vying for the same seat. Moi, whom I had the pleasure of meeting, was the much favoured candidate as the elections gathered pace.

There were two future notables serving in Baringo District during my spell in the area, Ruben Chesire of Kapasabet, and William ole Ntimama who hailed from Narok. Ruben went on to chair many a quasi-government enterprise and also served as a national MP, a friend to Moi he always was. William, after leaving the service was energised by politics through and through, to become a political 'war-horse' with many cabinet appointments to his credit. Once detained by Moi on incitement charges, he was released on a plea from his fellow tribesman, Edward Sokoine the Tanzanian PM. Doubt it not, Ntimama's epitaph has many shades.

These same two gentlemen in '63 were begging lifts to Nakuru in my beautiful red mercedes; their interesting company shortened the journey by far. But when the tables turned and their time arrived to collect their Mercs like flowers, I recalled our fleeting friendship from the past, to wonder about a lift from them in their brand new super cars. Sadly, at the time of this testimony, Ruben and William have left 'town' to enjoy their lives on a different plane, and may they rest in peace. They still remind me of that winding route we usually took from Kabarnet to Marigat, the iron bridge that crossed the Pekerra river, and the view of the sisal estates enroute to Kampi ya Moto. In those tougher times on unmade roads, a plume of murram dust was always there to mark our progress. Baringo District, part of the Great Rift Valley province, was a sisal farmer's paradise in places for Europeans and a scattering of locals, provided their farms were not near the rocky terrain of Kabarnet Boma. Vegetables and rocky hills were not ideal partners, and to emphasise this point there was always a shortage of cabbage in the boma, to make one share one's greens with the next-door neighbour lest the cooking smell revealed your selfish nature. Without electricity, power cuts were non-existent; the paraffin fridges with angled mirrors to eye the flame that eyes you back were few and far between, I certainly couldn't afford one. Fortunately for the masses, Tilley lamps were cheap to maintain and the main source of light after dark; pressurised paraffin ignited a silk mantle pre-heated by methylated spirits for the full light to appeared. Pumping to build up the pressure was the only 'pain in the neck.' And charcoal cooking jiko-style outside the kitchen door was normal practice. The second largest trading centre is Marigat, on the banks of a usually dried-up Chemeron river with a bed of stones to drain your driving skills; just before you take on the hair pin bends up the hill to Kabarnet. And let me not forget to mention the hot dry climate of Marigat, a natural onion-growing-area that thrives to this day. Close proximity to the lake also remains the right of the Njemps, who are very much in place as lakeside dwellers.

As long as anyone can recall, the Njemps living around Lake Baringo had been at loggerheads with the Tugen from Eldama Ravine (Moi's men). They wanted the lake to themselves and were prepared to fight for possession even before the Colonials came on the scene. Originally the Njemps were known as the Wa-Kwai and they lived around Lake Baro, but this has now all changed; the history of the 1890s is interesting but forgotten. However, the enmity between the 2 tribes was recognised by the Administration and sometimes used to pitch one tribe against the other; particularly so if a barrier had to be manned within the district. Of interest, Eldama Ravine rather than Nakuru was originally scheduled to become the HQ for the Rift Valley Province, however, the for and against remains debatable to this day.

During my time in Baringo the Island Camp was being planned, but had yet to become the tourist attraction it now is. In the meantime the lake was opened for fishing and the Luos had mind to catch the lot. They brought their boats from Kisumu and collected a permit to catch a specified quota, and the results came as no surprise; the lake was almost fished-out. The scheming plans of the Administration to use the local hate game between the two tribes had failed to control the size of the catch; fishing was therefore stopped. Setting the Tugen to check the Njemps hadn't worked after all, good old fashioned money had entered the fray and set the pace. Even the lakeside crocodiles were feeling the pinch without much fish according to Roberts, a Kampi ya Samaki lakeside dweller. He based his theory on the basking crocs with their mouths wide open and nothing to offer between their teeth. Their feathered friends were scarce and not about to fill in for the fish; pecking empty mouths was risky business. (see photo)

Baringo District was rugged by any standards; travelling in any shape or form had more than its fair share of hazards. Akoret, almost inaccessible by road, was to be my most distant polling station; it left a 10 mile trek to the southern shores of Lake Rudolf if one became adventurous. However, if you looked more deeply into this area, the sunny side was in the people themselves. The East Pokot Suk were adorned in the most elegant tribal regalia; (see front cover, a 75 year old today, and may God bless him.) pristine and titivated daily, it was part of their culture and more than a match in the bush for the modern day suits their brothers in the cities were dying to acquire.

Recently, colonial type tweed jackets, long wide-shorts, and funny settler hats, had become the rage and front page news in the local press. Questions were being tabled in the first parliament about such funny clothes worn by the new African farming elite. It was generally accepted that the old white settlers were a funny lot and wore extraordinary things, and I'm obliged to plead guilty when I see the picture of Peter and myself in front of his Citroen car. But why were these new farmers doing such things? Discussion about their farming attire also drew attention to the new suave suits in the halls of power worn by their newly elected brothers, who had used both hands to grab the white man's traditions; more or less like the new farming elite. It was a logical sequence of events and bound to happen according to the Suk when questioned on the subject, but they all agreed new fashions should be introduced at a more leisurely pace.

In the end, the confusion was such that all questions of dress were eventually left to the choice of the wearer; so the Saville Row suits of the Squires who hobnobbed with the Queen began to rule in the corridors of power. Such expensive tailoring was international and echoed the 'rags to riches' story of the newly elected MPs, born to rule and afford the best. They have now added a few extra spices to their own 'fashion pies'; bright red ties, bald macho heads and clear nail polish to challenge the manly set. The Kenya beaded-band, worn on wrists in national colours was also very useful to identify visitors and return them home if lost, while counting loot in overseas vaults. The new elite have at last arrived to out-shine the 'Marks & Spencer' suits of the High Commissioners'.

18

The 17th May 1963 was the actual date I mobilised my team in Baringo District to contribute to the national elections; the Kenyan image was at stake and we were determined to do them proud. The MPs, who would guide the country for the next 5 years were about to be elected; with opinions opined they were more than ready to occupy the first Independent Parliament. Excitement was in the air, history was in the making and I had caught the 'bug'. This was the year of the century and expectations were high, though for some their hopes would be dashed, while for others their wildest dreams were about to unfold; life was never fair, but that glimmer of hope for some was about to be fairer than most.

My team consisted of two long wheelbase Land Rovers, (see picture) several armed Tribal Police, two drivers, my cook, two clerks and myself. The drivers would also help the clerks to set up the polling-stations, induced by some extra cash for their efforts. The Tribal Police escort was armed with an assortment of weapons, a .22, .303, and a 12 bore shotgun, all of my personal choice. I had the Boma armoury key in my pocket and reasoned that the opportunity to live as a hunter-gatherer would not come around again, which roughly translated meant, the more my staff had to eat the greater my esteem; my ego was at stake and had to be fed along with our needs. Besides 'shooting for the pot' I had brought along half a sack of rice, 40lbs of posho (maize flour) for the camp and a bag of loose tea with ten pounds of sugar, all paid from my pocket; additions like milk and cabbage could be foraged on the way.

Philemon arap Chelego was my cook; a surprisingly thin young fellow he was, when cooks were usually pictured as short and fat and well fed from your personal larder, but whatever his physique Philemon was one of the best and I liked him. In the end he got wise and went to work for Vice President Moi in Kabarnet Gardens with my blessing, at treble the salary I could ill afford to match. He also had many mouths to feed. (see the picture he sent me at a later date) But in the meantime, he exercised his considerable talents with safari cuisine for my benefit. He had proved his worth on many occasions by fighting off snakes on over-hanging branches in make-shift kitchens, not to mention the hungry rats at floor level. He was an absolute gem by any standards and always produced a palatable plate of food for the evening meal. I never asked him what he was cooking before hand; it just turned up with a knife and fork on a china plate; no tin plates for me, and no thought of a spoon for everything African style. I acknowledge my finicky attitude, but what else do you have in the bush to embellish a meal other than shiny accoutrements.

On the eve of the elections, 6 merry men, each with his own team, spent the night assembled in an old wooden house in the Marigat centre; since an early start was required next morning. Well, that was the plan originally, but as a result of sharing accommodation, we became victims of our own cooks bragging between themselves about their 'Bwanas' being able to eat hotter food than the next, whereupon an extra handful of chillies would be added to the personal curry their hero was expected to eat. Each of us was carrying our own food supplies for separate cooking, but the spices for the evening were shared.

The cool beers from the local dispensary fridge hit the spot that night, working wonders to sooth our burning throats and other parts. But whatever the cure for the moment, we were all 'on fire' the next morning and somewhat delayed by our 'calling-cards' left behind in the local facilities. A sluggish mood then prevailed as I packed up to leave, with the daunting prospect of squatting in bushes when the pains returned. It really wasn't the squatting that was the big deal, but the wry smiles on the askaris' faces piqued my pride as I re-appeared. My cook in the meantime, would have been promoted to 'king' for his inner knowledge about my discomfort.

"I added a little bit of this and a little bit of that to my Bwana's food." Philemon would have explained with a mischievous smile. As I downed a beer the very next evening, I smiled in retrospect with my aggravation now hidden in the Baringo bush; I urge you, be careful where you step.

We dispersed from Marigat at about 9.30 am and headed towards the West side of Lake Baringo and Akoret, my first polling station. It was miles to the north of Nginyang and just below Lake Rudolf. A parched landscape and shifting sands in riverbeds lay ahead; in many cases vehicle tracks led up to the riverbank and the sand surface was pristine, which was sufficient reason to carry ropes to haul us out. But before we got stuck we would walk the dry riverbeds to test the looseness of the sand or wade in fast waters if the currents were strong. When I say we, it was usually someone hitching a lift who was obliged to take the walk or plunge, if he wanted to ride with us. We would then wait for him to shout for help if the current was too strong, and then look for another spot to cross where the flows were weaker. But to put your minds at rest, we never lost a passenger, though we thought it wise to keep an extra in reserve just in case. And why play the hero, when 'volunteers' are on hand to do the job.

Thorn trees upon impenetrable thorn trees were on either side of our rocky track; they were placed strategically by nature to herald our progress with a screeching and scratching against the vehicle paintwork. We got used to knowing the general direction by keeping an eye on the skyline; the same tactics our drivers used even before the roads got washed away. But to be absolutely sure, we relied on the local moran (warriors), who wanted a lift and knew the area since birth. Only one problem then remained, our vehicles couldn't climb trees and they were usually too wide for the tracks they wanted us to follow, but in the end we survived and are here to tell the tale.

We had been on the road for about 2 hours when I met the DC Lodwar, Charles Ryland. A wide brimmed safari hat, safari waistcoat with multiple pockets, shorts and Bata boots summed him up completely; I wasn't so differently dressed myself. His truck had a broken crown wheel and pinion and was abandoned in the general direction in which we were headed. Poor chap he certainly was, with his one and only Land Rover on his way to Marigat looking for help. I couldn't assist because I had my own schedule to keep, but I promised to signal the position of his truck to the Marigat garage from the police post at Nginyang to get a rescue underway. He had two days to reach Maralal and resume his election programme and the heavy vehicle workshop in Marigat was only 3 hours away, all things seemed possible. I never did hear the end of his story, but the purpose of my own schedule was to collect as many votes as I could. I occasionally stopped roadside to increase my tally, illegal may be and not gazetted, but who was to know, and a vote is a vote wherever? I also adjusted my polling times to fit in with the rhythmic humming of the 'bees' in the distance, which told of Suk itching to vote. The two most striking features of the Suk to impress, were their tiny wooden stools they carried everwhere to use in many different ways. As a seat, (see photo) or as a neck rest to preserve their elaborate hair styles; originally copied from the Karamojong. They also performed 'elephant' and 'ostrich' dances, which were almost obsolete at the time of the elections. Whether they are preserved in history today, I dare not hazard a guess?

After refuelling at Nginyang we pressed on to Kapedo. Once in its stride, our bush-bashing surmounted tortuous rocks and circumvented cactus plants with grey-green trunks. It's a god forsaken land until you blink and realise its beauty; cleansed by the arid and flushed by the floods it's alive to your senses. I switched off the engine for a moment to feel the serenity of the landscape. The height of the anthills that pock-mark the terrain are beyond belief; their cylindrical towers built layer upon layer, ring upon ring, oversee evolution from a privileged position due to the skills of the tiny termite. Floods transform the skyline and the anthills stand firm to match the strength of the rocky hills they challenge with every storm. These monoliths appear as the future designed by nature, to blaze the way for the 'Dubai towers' copied from the African bush. The anthills of Baringo are some of the tallest and thinnest free-standing termite towers in the world, and I for one was honoured to sense their image on my way to Akoret. (see photo) The beauty of the scenery, far outweighed the non-existent road that played the lurching game from one boulder to another. In the roughest areas distance was measured in time rather than mileage, the roads or lack of them dictated the progress. I quickly learned not to believe my guide's estimation given to please; distance, time and toughness of track was my thinking. To arrive an hour on either side, seemed a fair estimation.

We reached Kapedo at three in the afternoon. A collection of shanty huts in the distance bore the name of the village and looked positively hazardous, so I kept my distance and pitched camp in the vicinity of the hot sulphur falls; (see photo) used by Somali visitors to take of their healing qualities. Whether or not I had frightened away the usual crowd I wasn't to know, but the area of the falls was deserted that evening and the isolation was perfection. The actual sulphur-springs took the form of a waterfall flowing into a small river, so I eased myself under the cascade with a few prickly vines to challenge my comfort. Once settled, I was able to observe the confluence of the hot and cold flows and the small fish jumping out of the water to reverse their passage back into cold of the river. These 'tiddlers' were almost too small for human consumption, but the Egyptian geese were taking an interest in such tiny morsels; not too small for them I hasten to add. In turn, I was taking an interest in the Egyptian geese that were about the right size to feed the camp. Huge birds they were, and in my reckoning, one was sufficient to feed 6 hungry people.

As I dried myself off from the cascading falls, the sun was setting behind the indigenous trees that had escaped the charcoal trade. I then called for my 'fateful', or perhaps I should say 'faithful' 12 bore with SSG charges; a lethal weapon that was used in the emergency by the tribal police and home guards. These 'guys' the geese, were about to tuck themselves up for the night squatting 'safely' on an outstretched branch in the trees. However, their silhouettes against a chequered red sky meant that even an idiot could pick them off like flies; an idiot such as I! Four birds went to heaven that night and they were not on the wing when I shot them; unsporting maybe, but we needed to eat; two were kept for the following night.

Though I didn't realise it at the time, my team were natural cooks to a man and they didn't mess with the niceties of 'Hells Kitchen', TV style. By the way, the curse of the 'TV box' in Kenya had yet to arrive in serious form at that time. In Baringo that evening as the darkness closed in the stillness of the African bush encouraged the stars to twinkle, but nobody cared for their beauty; the scent of the cooking was in the air and the meat of the moment was all that mattered. The fire was building up nicely, the goose was divided and each man had a piece on a personally crafted stick. Like all good things, the blazing fire, the goose, the intention of cooking and eating, were all well tuned; we watched and waited for the first aromas to excite our senses. Sweaty facial expressions showed an eagerness to eat, gleaming white teeth were itching to squeeze the juices from their hand held morsels. In the meantime, the meat was left to sing an 'aria' all of its own; it sizzled in the air and fizzled on the fire and the lip-smacking of the cooks joined in the chorus; only a sprinkle of salt was needed.

As the drama unfolded, some cooking was followed by a thorough inspection; the glowing embers had yet to yield the final touches. Philemon, my man, did his stuff on my behalf; I didn't want to interfere with the men's natural humour among themselves, and my esteem had never been higher. A warm beer helped the meat go down when it was finally cooked, but for me it was tough though sweet for the others, if their chat was anything to go by.

We left early for Akoret the following morning, to open the polling station by 10 am in the Chief's two-roomed office. For reasons I have yet to understand, elections energised customs, personalities, and some fierce acting designed to scare the pants off me! I didn't know what it was all about and what to expect, but after a few more charges by the moran with spears held menacingly at the ready my nerves began to fray. These guys were enjoying the white man's fear, and it showed; as their enjoyment and my fear joined the ceremony. The Chief who'd been collecting my empty .22 cartridges to fill his ear lobes then deigned to reassure me, 'show no fear', he said, 'hapana ogopa', were his very words.

"It's our custom to show our courage on special occasions, we'll soon get on with the voting," I took a deep breath and reset my thinking.

Another rush then followed and the loud chanting stopped as they reached the door of the booth; by design they were almost at attention and waiting to vote, their spears planted firmly in the ground. Sharp pointed pliable blades about 8 feet tall were glinting like freshly honed steel as they reflected the morning sunlight. I wouldn't like to be on the end of one of those was my thinking at the time, that's where my enemies should be! I kept such thoughts to myself for them not to get any ideas. The moran 'advanced guard' had arrived early and this was the first contingent according to the Chief, who assured me the whole clan were on their way and intent on voting. As though to prove him right, a deep humming sound began to resonate in the valley. Softly at first, it gathered strength as they came into view. Spears were again thrust forward and then wrenched back in time to the rhythm; during this movement they were held upright in military side-arms fashion. The women and children followed with an occasional baby strapped on the back, all wanted to get in on the act.

A spokesman stepped forward and whispered something in the Chief's ear, and he in turn whispered something in mine. They wanted advice about voting for a suitable person and my driver looked as though he knew a thing or two, would I mind if they held discussions with him about the issue. I didn't want to know about the driver's preference and there were no agents to offer advice, so I told him to consult with them in the bushes and answer their queries as best he could without too much bias. I suspect his own candidate then got all the votes, but I wasn't to know. The tally reached 82 by 12 pm and the area was now deserted. I told the Chief if any one else wanted to vote they must report to Kolowa the following day, where I would be open for business just north of the Tugen hills. The pink indelible ink that was used to dip the 'pinkie', smallest finger when voting, had proved a great success. Every pool in the area was crimson; feathers, white shukas, and even head stools also showed a tinge of pink by the time I moved on. Occasionally, a second dip in the ink was requested and given to a favoured few, supplies were plentiful.

The driver stopped suddenly, and when I asked why, he assured me we had arrived at Kolowa and that was the Chief's office over there; he pointed to a small collection of mud-huts and a couple of stone buildings. It was early afternoon when I told my people to pitch my tent in the sandy river bed; it seemed to offer the best site away from the crowd. I waved the flies from the Chief's face as he told me his name; I genuinely wanted to see his expression, and as if on cue he also took up the waving to see whom I was; from thereon in we were friends.

He said I was not the only one who wanted to recognise the other when we next met; he also wanted to know what I looked like. I was the only White for miles around and as far as I can remember, there were only a couple of flies on my nose at the time, trying to fertilise eggs. I'm pleased to report that we did actually recognise each other later that evening without the waving; by then, the whine of the mosquitoes had replaced the buzz of the flies.

These flies by day travelled around in swarms; where the hell they all came from I had no idea and neither had anyone else. As soon as my tent was pitched, I sat on my camp bed under the mosquito net and called for my tea, always served in a china tea pot with matching cup and saucer. It was one of my hang-ups to enjoy a little luxury in the bush; 'Royal Albert, Old Country Roses' gave me much pleasure in the using. The china trio, a bed, a mosquito net, and a small box on which to place my essentials was far removed from the customs of the explorers at the turn of the century, who carted whole canteens of cutlery with fine glassware to match their Sherries; they also dressed for dinner. Nevertheless, in an impoverished kind of way, I thought I did rather well considering the falling standards. How the early explorers supped their tea I know not, but my style was to tap the spout to make sure the flies were out and about on other peoples bums and faces. But in spite of this action, there were always a few stragglers that floated out of the spout into my cup as I poured the tea. They would then haul themselves up my finger in bedraggled fashion to be flicked away; they weren't worth squashing with so many friends about. After my tea ritual, I walked over to the Chief's office to settle the voting arrangements for the following morning. He gave me the news that my visit had been passed around by word of mouth so I could expect a few extras, in addition to him and his staff; he also confirmed my thinking about the desolation of the place.

Later that evening when all the flies had shut up shop for the night, I ventured out beyond the confines of my tent once more; it was then that I discovered the true sanctity of the area when I stumbled upon a monolith to mark the site of the Kolowa massacre in the 1950s. According to the writing etched in stone, lives had been lost when tempers flared between local warriors and the tribal police. My recollection is that, 34 souls had gone to heaven on that fateful day. Regrettably, I was so wrapped up in the elections, I failed to take a picture of that special memorial.

I hope my inconsideration that evening doesn't lead to a little bit of history being lost in the now called Baringo County. To those who are interested, I recommend a visit to take the picture I failed to take. An inscription is worth its weight in gold if the memorial hasn't been defaced "ISIL style", by hate for history Kenya style.

When I awoke the next morning, I was feeling decidedly seedy as I swung my feet to the floor, blaming the local donkey for neighing all night. It was 6 am and Philemon was making tea. He asked if I would like an omelette with a couple of eggs that were always available, in addition he produced some white bread in waxed paper from Elliot's Bakery, Nakuru. In the meantime, I went for a wash in the crystal clear water produced by nature passing through sand, cool and refreshing it certainly was, no soap to contaminate was used. On my way back to the tent I saw crocodile tracks similar to the lakeside and Philemon confirmed them as genuine; he'd seen them when we first arrived and now he was enjoying my fear. He then said, he gets our tea water from the same pool but doesn't go there himself, it's too dangerous; so he sends the askari with a bucket, who doesn't know about the Croc.

True to the Chief's prediction, he and his staff voted that morning, and a couple of stragglers turned up around noon just before a resonant humming was heard in the valley, a repeat of the Akoret rhythm. The formalities by now were familiar to everyone in our team, the rhythm, the charging moran, the shaking and threatening with spears and the planting of weapons outside the booth. This time the driver's opinion was not sought and in the end we bagged 240 votes, our largest tally so far. The only negative to hit us that day was the late voters, which meant we had to remain in this fly infested area for another 12 hours, with the laughing donkey, and the crocodile we feared but had yet to see. So for a second time I shared the pool with the absent croc as I washed, followed by a couple of eggs on the last slice of Elliot's bread. By 10am we had struck camp and were travelling in the direction of Nginyang.

On route we stopped at Chipanda and collected 5 roadside votes just a few miles north of Churo, which we eventually reached via Tanglebwei at about 1.30 pm. For once our road conditions were reasonably good, obstructed only by scrub and small thorn bushes that our vehicles always took in their stride. The Chief at Churo was delighted to see my armed askaris clamber out of the vehicles, and the reason soon became apparent. Wild animals had carried off one of their cattle the previous night, a cow to be precise, and the camp was still in shock and talking about the roaring lions in their midst, whether one or two was not quite clear. But for sure they'd lost one cow and a milking one at that. Eventually they found the half eaten carcass when circling vultures reported the loss, but there was really nothing I could do about the threatening lions, other than help them sleep more soundly that night, with armed askaris on the spot.

The following morning, the local school was used for voting while the dispensary fridge cooled my evening beer. It had been tough in Akoret and Kolowa where this cooling arrangement was lacking, and the heat of the day demanded such as the sun went down, but a beer is a beer whatever the temperature, tasty and wet on the tongue. And in spite of the word 'imperial', that wreaked of things some loved to hate, the drinking of beer from imperial bottles continued long after independence.

After the voting at Churo, we continued to Nginyang the next day around noon, not withstanding some Baringo hazards enroute. Safaris were always challenging, if one part of the journey goes well you can bet your life there's a problem ahead, which in this instance forced us to remove the fan belts to cross a flooded river, after the waters waded reached armpit levels. Fan belt disconnection came with the experience of churning water under bonnets and flooded engines. Unfortunately, it took time to perform the mechanics, but it was an effort well worthwhile to avoid getting stuck in midstream. Finally, we reached another school where polling was scheduled for the following day, a couple rooms had been cleared for our operation.

Absolute luxury was mine for the taking that evening; had you been there you'd have known I was blessed. My tent was pitched on a purpose-built concrete plinth, water was available from a tap, my beer was cooled in a dispensary fridge, and only a token number of flies had turned up to share my meal. We were in such civilised circumstances that Philemon had actually set up my collapsible table in front of the tent, with a beer for the pouring into an ancient glass-bottomed pewter mug; the more ugly it was, the less likely it was to get broken. The 'film director's chair', better known as a standard folding camp-chair to most, was then planted firmly behind the table to creak and groan as I shaped the canvas to fit my bottom. Not quite the luxury of the new parliamentary 'benches' in the present day, but I knew my position in life; whether in the African bush or seated in town.

Two minutes later a long queue of locals formed to look me over; at the same time they wanted to present me with some complicated problems by way of a test. I tried to explain that I was only the fellow conducting the elections, but they weren't deterred. The general theme presented that evening was one of neglect by their future rulers, who hadn't been seen for months. I suspected such sentiments were expressed to curry favour with me rather than the actual facts, so I enjoyed my evening and played along with the guile of the guys on the ground at Nginyang. They did their best to squeeze an opinion from a worn out colonial relic, whom they knew was out on his neck after the elections.

A Headman then graced our gathering and began to blame all politicians, who had been too busy looking after 'George' (themselves) and were too greedy to help anyone else. 'George was George' is a figure of speech, and no one in particular, but in their eyes he was the man to blame. Selfishness was responsible for their lot in life and 'George' was the one who had caused their poverty. He then used a different idiom to explain his idle chatter, but when the ghost of George was re-introduced the crowd cheered loudly. I was left confused, with a me too from you, I suppose?

For the gathering, the Chief had placed his own chair to the right of my table and everyone else was obliged to stand, lean against a tree, or sit on the ground. No women were present; it was a man's business in those days and nothing appeared amiss to the men; least of all the women. Awkward questions about female representation had yet to be aired; the year was 1963 and the men of the tribe were real men without a thought for the firewood gatherers, water carriers and baby bearers. In any case, they had already told their women how to vote and that was the end of the matter. Casting couch sex to get a part in the movies was in the future and the men of this time still beat their wives once a week, or if the food didn't please. Full-blown sex without the prelude of pinching bottoms it always was, but the women were in pensive mood, their time was coming and overdue. As usual everyone wanted a say, from the headmen in khaki bush jackets with traditional beaded head gear, to those who spent their lives chasing cattle thieves and avoiding taxes. And finally the wise old men, who enjoyed negotiating dowries.

The headmaster of the local school claimed to have received a collection of desks and benches for his pupils, only to add a story about the money for the building having disappeared. He pointed towards a huge tree under which the furniture was sitting with no building in sight, a sad state of affairs and no doubt the DC knew about it, but nothing was going to happen, nothing ever did. Nevertheless, I made a note and he seemed satisfied that I would pass on the information for speedy redress, what else could I do? To them I was there on administrative duties rather than voting procedures, and I don't deny I welcomed the opportunity to hear their views on other issues, my knowledge of which was sadly lacking.

After about an hour, the Chief who'd been nodding support to the many opinions from the crowd, announced the elections the following morning in the local dialect; I then closed the meeting in due haste before anyone else stood up to prolong the session. At last my trial was over and the evening now belonged to me; a brand new experience was about to be mine. As the moon rises above the trees a determined cold sets in and the water in my canvas bath almost turns to ice. I still shudder to this day as I recall that freezing moment when I took the bath of a lifetime in the African bush; an experiece not to be repeated, I hasten to add.

As the hairpin bends wind their way up the hill from Marigat to Kabarnet, the weight of my safari begins to lift from my shoulders; I'm almost home and dry with a precious store of memories for my dotage in the years to come. Finally, I hang up my boots on the 26th May 1963 at 4 pm, having left Nginyang around noon with a final tally of 1401 out of a possible 1700 on the register. At that moment in time I'm morally indebted to the Kenya government and North Baringo for a unique adventure that stretched experiences to the extreme. To beg the question, would I wish to repeat this exercise all over again, who knows, food for thought remains with me.

After all my efforts Daniel Toroitich arap Moi was duly elected to serve in the first parliament of a newly Independent Kenya. Who then would have foreseen his fantastic future; 24 years as President of Kenya, ivory baton in hand, no holds barred.

19

Nakuru town and the national independence celebrations off Langata Road Nairobi, was but 100 miles apart; and to witness the striking of the new Kenya flag was my intention entirely. My special friend in Nakuru was a feisty nurse from the European Hospital, Pat Smith by name and she hailed from the Isles of Jersey. For all I knew, she could have been injecting all and sundry for miles around, but our common thought for the night of the 12th was an effortless ride to the capital city. In December '63 it was only a matter of a couple of hours on a sparsely occupied road to reach the venue before the strike of midnight; a simple trip describes it well.

Newly-dug bench terracing was evident just off the old Langata Road, specially constructed to support our weight with thousands of others. We were about to view the spectacle of the century from a position of utmost clarity, it was ours for the taking. We, the insignificant few, were grandstanding sufficiently to recognise the VIPs one by one; heads of state were in the background, Mzee Kenyatta and the Duke of Edinburgh were centre stage. The show was theirs; Mzee was charming the crowds and urging them on by flicking his fly-whisk, all eyes were on him and his presence spoke volumes, he was the star of the show.

To add to our own selfish pleasures that evening, licensed car drivers were scarce on the roads. They were still in their formative years, and may God bless them, before they move from their donkey cart driving behind the behind of a donkey, to behind the wheel of a limo from the land of the rising sun.

Prince Philip, was resplendent in white naval uniform with sash and dress sword, and Mzee Kenyatta, ever the showman, wore his beaded fez in national colours and held his fly-whisk at the ready. It is said that Philip enquired of Jomo, as they stood side by side with the remaining seconds ticking away.

"Do you want to change your mind?"

It was then that Jomo's jovial mood exploded into laughter for the evening to hit new highs; the timing was perfect and the lights went out. Next thing we knew the flag was struck on the dot of midnight, the band played the National Anthem, fireworks rent the air and the crowds exploded with joy urged on by tribal dancing; the night belonged to all who were there. The terrace where we were standing was wet and muddy with a light rain falling, but the very nature of the people pushed back the weather for this great occasion; all loved the moment and shared the vibrations. During that very same morning, with the birth of a nation fixed in our minds, we journeyed back to Nakuru. Sadly, there are but a handful of privileged Kenyans now living who actually stood on that spot off the Langata road on the 12th December when history unfolded, though many may claim they were there as kids to ease their cravings for that wonderful night when Kenyatta's dreams came true.

Nairobi City Hall was the biggest venue in town; nothing much had transpired since Sir Evelyn Baring had declared it open in 1957, other than the missing plaque from the wall commemorating his efforts. The hall had been waiting for years for something huge to happen, and the wake-up call arrived with independence. Ironically, the very symbol of authority that had declared City Hall open and the Mau Mau rebellion to be a threat, was now party to the party through a third party; the Duke no less, who was there to bless the occasion. Wishful thinking some fifty years on was a misty vision at the time, but open your eyes today, look around, development takes one's breath away. After much celebrating, the new year dawned for the euphoric highs to give way to running the country. As for me, 1963 was a milestone in my life; I was on a roll in my own small way and 'things' were moving, the vibrations were there.

Being a mere mortal, I didn't expect to be invited to the Ball of the Century, though I had many friends with that honour behind them. Grace Wagema, with a degree in home economics from Howard, USA was one of the favoured few; her VIP sister Jane was married to the first African permanent secretary for labour, Meshak Ndisi. So I was not surprised to find her with a souvenir cigarette box from that very special evening. Sizewise, it held 50 cigarettes of the Players Clipper brand, a top seller at the time. The box was made of cedar wood, bearing the Kenya Coat of Arms in coloured enamel affixed to the lid. It is a collector's item by any standards today, so if you have one lying at home consign it to the National Museum, where visitors need to pause for thought.

Mzee, the Duke, Indira Gandhi, and a youthful Aga Khan were in the chairs occupied by the 'heavies'; others of lesser ilk were either standing or in small groups sharing smaller tables and redpadded chairs aplenty. In the eyes of the radio commentator, the ladies were the stars of the show that night; they were dressed to kill for this once in a lifetime celebration.

1500 guests, give or take a few, occupied City Hall that evening, a third of which at any one time were doing 'The Twist', the dance craze of the night. Pushing the physical limits as Kenyans always do, they were twisting themselves into knots to match the movements of a certain young lady, Muthoni Likimani's daughter no less, had the old men turning back the clock. She was tall and slender and easily got down, went round and round and up and down, but when the copycats got down and couldn't get back up, the on-lookers revelled and enjoyed the ball even more! Harry Bellafonte and Miriam Makeba were in top form and enthralled the guests with their signature tunes. Radio listeners, myself included, enjoyed the relayed merriment courtesy of commentator Timothy Bungey; it was early morning and we were left straining for more.

As post independence gathered pace, the guys in my office on genuine leave grew beards, and my souvenir arrows I used for decoration began to disappear. What exactly they had in mind, I had no idea, but eventually their pictures appeared in the local press as forest fighters looking for their 'fruits of independence'. 'Fruits' being the operative word, was in capital letters. Precious land had been the aim of their scheming, and why not they asked the questioning crowd? When my hard working office staff saw their pictures and heard the news in the local press about their activities, they returned to the office as heroes, having tried their luck and lost; though the very fact they'd used such a ploy drew admiration aplenty. Apparently, they had enjoyed their leave in association with some genuine fighters, who much like them had come away with nothing. Whilst the new elite, who took the land, had neither beards nor arrows; they sat behind their loyalist desks and shuffled title deeds.

We are still in Nakuru and George Sutton the Provincial Accountant is my immediate boss; he was not exactly 'my cup of tea' and little humour was ever exchanged between us. However, as Jagdish and I, his underlings, were out of the office most of the time, personal feelings were of little concern. Doubtlessly, George was an upstanding dour man, though for the whole of my two years in that office we never made social contact, I mixed with others of a more outgoing nature.

Ray and Edith Batchelor, with Christen and Clare their tennis star daughters, were a delightful Nakuru family to know. And luck favoured me when I joined them on the SS Uganda from Mombasa to Tilbury Docks London in 1964; those were lazy laid back days, and for once I wasn't expected to arrive before I set out. En route we docked in Aden for duty-free goods, and then casually sailed on to Suez, where we boarded a bus for Giza, a camel ride and a bit of pyramid climbing inside and out. I have to admit the size of the blocks on the outside were too daunting for me in my healthy state to think of reaching the top; halfway and maybe not that, was my limit. We re-boarded the ship at Port Said via the Cairo Museum and the Hilton Hotel where we lunched in absolute luxury; the golden pillars in the dining room paid homage to us and the Pharoes at the same time. The Bensons, Pam and Chris from the Machakos era were also in our crowd, complete with a set of lively twins, Martin and Jackie, life-long friends to this day.

Ray Batchelor, an ex SAS military man and the Provincial Sports Officer Rift Valley, had at one time played football in the Premier League; West Ham United was his team. In those days they were paid £8 a week compared to £60,000 today; without doubt he would have been a millionaire had his timing hit the spot. Ray always had a good tale to tell involving his sporting colleagues, who were always jostling among themselves to reach the ultimate; an elected MP. Sports organisations and labour unions were the hottest positions in town to climb the ladder to fame in those early days. Elbows were always flaying to get to the front of the queue, and to hell with the voters after the ballot, was the accepted form. Imagine, at first you're at the front of the queue to get into a lift, then you're at the back and the overloading sounds as you step inside. These guys were seriously hungry for power and manners didn't exist, so be mindful of the tsunami or get trodden under foot when queuing in town, or anywhere else for that matter.

With independence, Majimboism or regionalism was born. The President of Great Rift was the Honourable Daniel Toroitich arap Moi, and his secretary the Provincial Commissioner was Jack Wollf. The new establishment led by the Honourable Moi was paid by my office and he topped the list at Shs 1700 per month in the form of a cheque, which he promptly exchanged for cash. The other members of the Regional Assembly received Shs 600 per month; the cheque issued to them was also exchanged for cash. Why didn't I pay cash in the first place you may well ask, but a cheque to me was a more dignified way to pay salaries to our new bosses; that was my thinking, unappreciated at the time.

Emperor Haile Selassie and Mzee had always been the greatest of friends, and by way of cementing their friendship Mzee had given a building plot to Selassie soon after independence. As a result, the new Ethiopian Embassy was built on State House road in a much favoured position. His Royal Highness was even shorter than Mzee and twice as thin, and that's my excuse for missing his person when they were wowing the crowds in Nakuru. I did however manage to capture their 'chariot' on film in the form of a beautiful white Lincoln Continental Coupe, a gift from the American people at Independence.(See picture).If you peer more closely, you will espy the back of Selassie's peak cap, though his face and his ever-present dog called Lulu is missing.

Talking about cars in Nakuru, I find it difficult not to mention Bob Pittway's experience late one night on the Nakuru-Nairobi road. Bob was a true friend by any standards and at the time of this story I'm about to recount, he was the key-man in the Exchequer and Audit, Rift Valley Province. His discoveries pinpointing shortages and an occasional rare surplus were so important that, the Minister of Finance James Gichuru would refer to his efforts in parliament. I have an open invitation to visit Bob on his home turf in the middle of the Irish Sea. The Isle of Man from whence he hails, awaits my exploration. Bob was a brilliant investigator, but sometimes a bit rash in real life; check this out for yourselves. Vandals, I'll call them vandals, though much stronger language would better describe such devils at work that night when stones began to fly in Bob's direction. He'd slowed down at the time to negotiate a bend in the road at the Diatomite mining project, he was on his way back

from Nairobi. This shower of stones was a first time experience for Bob and he couldn't believe it was happening; it was then that his auditing mind decided to recheck the facts as he would do in his profession. He turned his car around and went back to the scene for confirmation, only to receive another volley of stones as he passed the same spot for a second time. By then he was on the Nairobi side of the stone-throwing vandals, and so far, all the 'bricks' had missed.This story was recounted to me the very next morning, having parked his American car with the shattered windscreen outside my office. The first question he asked was, where can I get another screen, for which he felt obliged to offer an explanation. Apparently, on his third pass to regain the Nakuru side of his attackers they found their range, hence the broken glass. His foot then hit the floor to leave the rogues in shock. That's how he told his story fresh that morning, before embellishment Kenya style, crept in, to make his plot unique.

20

Nairobi

The year is 1966 and I'm on the move again. My worldly possessions are squeezed into my car and Nakuru is about to be left behind forever. The Capital City is in my sights. I shall be working for Peter Shiyukah, my friend and mentor from our Kitale days in '62. As Permanent Secretary, Ministry of Lands and Settlement, Peter had arranged for my transfer from the Provincial Administration to his Nairobi portfolio. His prior position of Provincial Commissioner Nyanza, was now in the capable hands of Charles Murgor, originally from the African Courts in Nakuru.

The cards were stacked in my favour and I held four aces, life was truly on my side; for the second time in my civil service career a person who handled figures from my London days was needed in town; the figures on high heels I'll keep to myself for the moment. With no modesty involved, Nairobi was dying for my company and the crowds would be lining the route, so I dared to believe. My time had come and Peter had picked the right man for the job; his trust in me I was about to return a hundred fold.

I was duly appointed Assistant Secretary Finance and Personnel and immediately began to move in august circles, hitherto beyond the reach of my humble station in life. I was now socialising with the headline makers, the movers and shakers in the daily news from Alliance High; all due to Peter's friendship and introductions. My new associates were mostly beautiful people with only a sprinkling of 'artful-dodgers', gobbling land and property.

From the fleeting table etiquette lessons at the Kitale Hotel, which was my *place in the sun* with Peter and Eluid Mahihu, I was about to learn how to play the game as the *new boy* in town. My place at the *new top table* made me listen to Peter's words of wisdom. He would say… 'if you want something urgently make sure you're in the driving seat, because when you're told no problem, you can bet your life there is one'. Furthermore, he advised… *the come back on Monday syndrome* can go on forever, so nip it in the bud before it gets out of hand. And never forget the golden rule, the first bribe is always the cheapest.

The Ministry of Lands and Settlement occupied 3 floors of the Silo Park building on Queensway, now Mama Ngina street. As you came out of the lift on the ministerial floor there was a slothful telephone operator seated close-by, who from time to time got a wake up punch in the ear from Jesse Gachago, selfelected to be in charge of her discipline. When it worked no one complained, it was just the right medicine to straighten her out. In fact our girl was so bad at answering calls the Commissioner of Lands confessed to putting his receiver in an empty enamel bowl, his primitive office washing facilities, to listen at length to the ring-tone before she picked up; he continued with his office work in the meantime.

Whatever the pros and cons to liven up switchboard operators, the cure was surely doing the rounds; the PS in Treasury had also beaten his idling girl, but unfortunately for him, he hadn't reckoned on an irate husband. A punch-up then ensued in a treasury office to energize a circular from the Director of Personnel, Joe Githenge, to cool things down. After that, operators were put on notice to work with due diligence or get the sack in an orderly manner; a thump in the ear was no longer due process.

The switchboard saga had only lasted a few weeks, before another snake reared its ugly head from behind the office filing cabinets. It was called 'the scandal of the secretaries,' they were being chased around the office by their lustful bosses. And the minister was sufficiently moved to rule enough was enough, those involved would henceforth have male secretaries. And there was no question of 'gays coming out', we were still in the middle-ages, a man was a man and that's what they got. When these tricks crossed my desk they only served to brighten our day. Henry Kuria in his mischievous way likened such antics to taking the place of parliamentary sessions; the law makers were in recess for another two weeks and our love of humour was lacking its usual style.

The building opposite the 20th Century Cinema located our offices in the Silo Park. The Honourable Jackson Harvester Angaine was the minister, closely supported by his assistant minister, Honourable Jesse Gachago. The permanent secretary was Peter Shiyukah and his private secretary, a wonderful girl, was Ansuya Shah; just married when we last met. Aveling Abutti, a charming chap, was the deputy, and the under secretary was Arthur Davies husband to Patience, a medical practioner. The Assistant Secretaries were Ralph Palmer, finance and personnel, and my secretary was the long-suffering Satwant Panesar, a beautiful unflappable Sikh lady who typed the ministry estimates again and again until they were perfect. After that, the minister would then make his parliamentary appearance to get the budget approved. The final member of the team was Henry Kuria, assistant secretary administration, who hailed from Banana Hill where his outside activities were steeped in literature. The Tausi (peacock) Theatre Group was famous for using his original marriage proposal…'Nakupenda, lakini, mimi maskini. I love you, but I'm so poor.' Back then, it was a remarkable visionary forecast for fifty years hence; little did he imagine the transition from the Wamaskini (poor people) then, to the present day Masafaras.

The various heads of departments within the ministry were the Commissioner of Lands Jimmy O'Laughlin and his deputy Frank Charnley, Sidney Lock the Town Planning Adviser, Peter Anyumba the Director of Surveys and James Kinyanjui, who I see on occasion these days, was the Director of Land adjudication. Last but not least, a big wheel in the system was the Director of Settlement James Maina, now known as Maina Wanjigi, (a recent autobiographer; see Nyali Hotel photo) Maina was the only departmental head in the Silo Park; everyone else was spread throughout the town to preclude the ministry from breathing down their necks; doubt it not, we were equally grateful for the distance between us. The Minister parked his Humber Super

Snipe at the entrance to the Silo Park and the PS had parking in the building. Myself, I parked my red Volvo sports on the pavement under the lamp post to the rear of the building outside the bank. Cars and the hassle of parking was not the bane of one's life; we were in the mid 60s and it was more beautiful then. The messy rural masses oozing into the city were still small in number; slightly short of a million souls with many fingers in many pies, 'angaika...ing', busy with affairs defines the mood.

A future personality lying low in Lands at that time was Authur Magugu, son of a Senior Chief from Kiambu. He was known for his bushy hair and handsome features; his Peugeot 203 Coupe with canvas top helped his bachelor status to attract the beauties he wished to know. On occasion we would meet outside office hours before we both left the ministry and drifted apart. Unknown to me at the time, Arthur had ambitions that I was able to follow in the local press. When we next met he was Minister of Finance and a car pulled up as I was walking along Queensway. A voice commanded 'get in', his ministerial car was offering me a lift, a more polished guy you couldn't wish to meet.

Lands and Settlement was a tight-knit organisation and problems were quickly resolved by opening the doors of those who knew the answers; the 8th floor was our tenure. Sometimes, before work, we would meet up at The Coffee Shop across the road in Queensway, (now Mama Ngina) where on occasion I would also link-up with best friend Mohinder Dhillon of Africa Pix, a tenant in the 'Nairobi House' building of protected monument status. It was the original HQ for The British East Africa Company in 1910, a decade before colonisation in 1920.

Unfortunately, a recent depiction of this ancient building on our national stamps failed to preserve its place in Nairobi history, but Kipande House and the District Commissioners buildings still stand tall to remind of a past.

Alternatively, we chose the coffee place under our building for the big meet-up around 7.30 am. The white-man, that's me, would be expected to pay for the coffee based on the fallacy he had more money than anyone else; rumours most foul, but that was the thinking and my burden to bear. In actual fact, the locals had more money in their bank accounts at the beginning of the month, but they also had more relatives and hangers-on. When I stayed over with Peter in his father's Kakamega house, a brand new tractor draining the pocket of a dutiful son was in the garden as we brushed our teeth to start the day. Peter shrugged for a fleeting second and I understood why; it was one of those things in life he couldn't avoid, much like his new Citroen car to match his position in the civil service.

Before we ascended to the 8th floor of the Silo Park, an occasional story over coffee might emerge from the night before; and if told really well it could lift our spirits and lighten our thoughts for the rest day. Apparently, crooks were hitting the establishment; it was no longer safe to give a *lifti* in your car, no matter how pretty she was. Some chatter doing the rounds was about a fellow bundled out of his car in Doonholm road; fortunately for him he'd landed in front of a row of railway landhies. But on the minus side were his clothes; he was standing naked in a clean white vest. Bare feet from the roadside to the first front door was the easiest part of his problem, but deeper thought was needed when he knocked on the door to summon help; should he pull down the front of his vest to cover his you know what, and show his bottom to the passing crowd, or should he pull down the back and keep his personal details between him, the person answering the door and his wife. And there again, who was going to let him in without questions through a bolted door; his shouting was bound to attract attention. Finally, the poor fellow was rescued, but the event had left him scarred for life. One of the group having coffee then demonstrated lightheartedly how he would've tackled the problem, by grabbing the front and pulling the back through, between his legs. That was just one of many ideas mentioned that morning before we dispersed to the office, but by then our joyous laughter had become rather nervous, for a future *lifti*, to require much thought.

Lands and Settlement was the most powerful docket in the government; even more powerful than the Ministry of Finance and Defence lumped together. Lands even left the President out of breath when it came to controlling the registrar's office. As a national past-time and as long as anyone could remember, the grabbing of land and other peoples tribal chattels, women and cattle included, was a way of life before the British organised their own grabbing spree. Original land-titles were actually torn up when heated arguments got out-of-hand, and these same records are still missing. From the office messenger to the minister, those who owned land owned the country, and the niceties of queuing for a piece of the action were just not there. It was more like elbowing Kenya style into a bus or a lift, and stepping over the bodies to grab a bit of the action. Land grabbed by the Europeans was being grabbed back with a vengeance; every piece was justified as long as a true Kenyan swallowed it whole; railway sidings and traffic islands were on notice. Even sleeping on duty at police stations was not a good thing, if an unfenced patch of land was at the back.

No matter how big a European homestead was, the maximum price to be paid for any house bought within the settlement scheme was £6000. Sometimes the price of the house was left off the list by mistake or intention, and it then came for free. On one occasion I was asked by the lucky new landowner about their free house, and what they should do? Under the circumstances I suggested they give the government the option to remove it from their land, knowing full well nothing would happen. The gentry aimed to be 'Landed Gentry' colonial style, like the *Robber Barons* in Europe hundreds of years ago. The bigger the piece of the country they grabbed the more gentrified they became. In true Kenya fashion, the poor became poorer as they stood by and smiled at the nimble thieves, who robbed them before their very eyes. During my 3 years in the ministry, some of the 'biggies' had actually collected many many farms for themselves, almost free of charge, and true to form the forest-fighters got almost nothing; so unfair but abundantly true.

Being in the Ministry of Lands I was privy to mind-boggling documentation, which was but a small sample of the landgrabbing activities. I was merely a shell-shocked ringside spectator complete in my naivety, observing human greed at its best. My personal theory was that land in Kenya belonged to the African, but not just a few; it was there to be shared by the many. What nonsense was I thinking? Commerce was generally in Asian hands and the international companies were multi-racial. My humble appraisal entirely in the 60s, though time moves on and opinions change. There was a wise old man running the country, he was so wise that he knew exactly the importance of the Commissioner of Lands. No Kenyan in his time, and in particular one of his own tribe, would occupy that position, if he could possibly help it. But, unbeknown to Mzee, the scheming to unseat Jimmy O'Loughlin by devious means was in motion and about to succeed. Jimmy was a loyal employee and Kenyatta's right-hand man through and through, he would follow Mzee's instructions to the letter. So it was only by chance that an attempt on Jimmy's employment came to light. On this occasion, so I was told, a friend of Kenyatta wanted the plot next to the Standard Bank opposite the Stags Head Hotel in Nakuru, and when Jimmy took the call from State House a third-party was in the room, who could well have been his assistant, Frank Charnley. The conversation went something like this…

"Mister O'Loughlin," Kenyatta always called the Commissioner by name.

"Yes Sir?" O'Loughlin always called Kenyatta, Sir.

"I want you to meet me outside the Stag's Head Hotel in Nakuru when I'm there at the end of this month. I have someone in mind, who wants the vacant plot opposite the Hotel."

"I'm sorry Sir," came back the reply, "but at the end of this month I will be on 6 months leave pending my Africanisation. I'm proceeding on retirement."

"Aieee!" echoed down the line, loud enough to be heard in the centre of town. It was an alarming exclamation for Jimmy to hear, but he knew full well the meaning by intonation and volume alone. Mzee was annoyed, very annoyed indeed!

"Mister O'Loughlin, come and see me now!" Kenyatta was clearly alarmed that his Commissioner was on his way out, but at the same time he was rather pleased he had just caught the treachery in time. And sure enough, a simple letter landed on my desk later that day from Mzee, typed in huge print on his personal typewriter. It was a memorandum to the Ministry and confirmed Mister O'Loughlin in the position of Commissioner of Lands for a further period of 4 years. Kenyatta's personal signature in green ink, not ball point, laid down the law and the attempted coup was dead. The vacant plot in Nakuru was duly allocated, built upon and a bank moved in.

On return from home leave a few years into my future, I was to face a less momentous, but similar situation to that of the Commissioner. By then John Koitie was the new Permanent Secretary, an elegant figure and a gentleman all rolled into one. The Ministry hierarchy was changing and the new deputy secretary wasn't a patch on Avelyn Abutti the economics major, he replaced. He was far 'too clever' for himself and also for me; he began to interfere with my estimate work and I didn't like it. I told him so, and he resented my comments. Suddenly, I was to be Africanised; a formal letter was dropped on my desk to confirm the deputy secretary had been busy. It was then that I informed the Minister that I was about to proceed on leave pending retirement, when he asked me to draft his speech to declare a cattle-dip open. The notice was duly withdrawn with little fuss, but by then I was forewarned about the evil spirits in the air and I had no gecko from the tug boat captain in Tanga to protect my back. So six months later I decided to bite the bullet and leave of my own accord. George Chege, a petrol station owner from Fort Hall, Kirinyaga, and a civil servant all rolled into one, was about to step into my shoes; the time had arrived to dust-off my chair on the 7th floor of Jogoo House; new talent was desperately needed; my assessment entirely.

The capital city in the sun in the '60s, was not that congested. Quaint and countryfied almost fits the bill. To cross the city from boundary to boundary took no more than 15 minutes, and to think about where you worked and where you stayed was never in contention. Even the Kenya buses kept time and the conductor supervised the overcrowding with a certain amount of diligence. Boarding passengers mostly used the regular entrance, but on occasion they squeezed through the fire escape windows at the back to help the flow. If detected, they risked a blow on the head from the multi-task ticket machine, used to collect the fares and relieve passenger boredom. Instant retribution was always a lively affair; it induced much chuckling from those who warmed to the scene when a culprit was bundled off the bus. Those were happy days and no-one got shot, they merely collected a lump on the head for a couple of weeks, before they did it all over again. Unfortunately, such life is on the wane these days and live entertainment has now been replaced by modern music designed to blow your brains out, if any remain from the disco-blasts of the night before. It's called life in the fast lane, matatu-madness, and make sure you choose the seat in the middle to cheat the 'Pearly Gates' on the Kenya roads!

I checked into the nearest hotel that fitted the size of my pocket. Plums Hotel in Plums Lane off Oljijo Road in Westlands was my choice; a flat within the compound became my home for the next few years. This particular residence was also a pleasant backwater for the aged, who had managed to avoid the more institutional Harrison House, the alternative on the Nairobi scene. They were as free as birds and the tolerance practiced by Karim the owner had truly come from heaven; he listened to all their quirks. As for me, I never did find the reputed plums or even the trees for that matter, and my travelling time to the office in the Silo Park never exceeded a hand of minutes. The sprawling cluster of hotel buildings on either side of Plums Lane can lightly be described as a 'watering-hole' for a small European community, whose ancestry stretched from Belsen concentration-camp in Poland to Christchurch New Zealand; from Mr Olshosky to Miss Haybittle, two of the more genteel residents.

At the other end of Plum's society came Pinkie, the enginedriver from the north of England; a down-to-earth character as bald as a coot, who radiated a pink glow to match his name when exposed to the African sun. His moustachioed buddy called Frank had all the hair in the places where Pinkie had none, he also lodged at Plums. As working-class men who were bound to dirty their hands, Pinkie and Frank did not qualify to join Nairobi Club, but had their own Railway Club for their recreational purposes, similar to the Public Works establishment in Nairobi West. These were the days when different classes had different clubs to match their different comforts, such were the divisions in society when the colony was born. However, Pinkie and Frank were a happy-go-lucky team, and they shared the caboose at the end of the train when they travelled on duty to Kampala and Mombasa. Sometimes, such a situation was fraught with danger after a beer or two, if Pinkie's girl entered into the fray. It was then that the men stuck together and Wanjiku, poor Wanjiku, was tossed off the train when it travelled more slowly on one of the bends. But to give them their due, Wanjiku told me without any hard feelings, they always collected her at the nearest station to her point of departure on the way back. Well, that's how Wanjiku related the story, but one never knew if it were true, she was known to be such a liar.

Nevertheless, Pinkie had lived with his ageless Kikuyu girl for dozens of years, and to the careful observer a deep understanding existed between them, mutual love could be seen in their eyes by those who knew them well. Wanjiku was a clever girl, and from her mixing with Whites, she was even more fluent in English than her men appeared to be; she could swear like a trooper to express her feelings on many a subject. *Fucking hell* was her usual expression of incredulity; whether it was a badly cooked egg on her plate at breakfast or the car had a flat tyre… *fucking hell* would express Wanjiku's feelings, one way or another.

Miss Haybittle on the other hand, was a trim, prim, exschoolteacher, and her white, blonde curly hair was subject to an occasional perm by a visiting friend. Her face was weathered by time like mine is today, but she never forgot to pamper her cheeks with a pinkish rouge and always painted her lips a brightish red to keep up appearances. A dear lady by any measure she was, a gem from the Victorian era and patchwork quilts were her forte, large ones at that. On one occasion I was to witness the admiration of Miss Haybittle's work by Wanjiku, after she had declared the quilt to have more than 200 patches stitched together. Wanjiku was impressed and felt bound to express her admiration by using her favourite words, *fucking hell*, without a thought for the sensitivity of the artist and her needlework. A coughing and spluttering was Miss Haybittle's reply, and the ever-thoughtful Wanjiku slapped her on her back oblivious to the cause. Wanjiku had a good heart; she was a lovely girl who had just picked up a few bad habits from these rough tough working-class men from the north of England. She was almost one of them when it came to language, but on occasion her fluency was subject to a slip of the tongue when the amazing happened to blow her away. Miss Haybittle for some reason, was her fascination and admiration all rolled into one.

When my mother Alice, who was one of the youngest

old ladies visiting 'Plums' met Miss Haybittle, she was in her element discussing her native Australia over afternoon tea following a rubber of bridge, with those who possessed the bidding skills. Such happenings were late in my government service; I'd been living at 'Plums' on and off for so many years by then, I could well have been part of the fixtures.

As life progressed there was little doubt that 'Plums' was solely in the hands of Karim, a pillar of the Ismaili Community. And his cross to bear in life was the welfare of the aged Europeans in limbo at the time of independence. Benevolence was his byword, and he handled this group of elderly dignified people with care and consideration, knowing full well they'd lived better lives in better times. They were now 'his responsibility' as they waited for their time to depart… they were lost souls with small pensions and little savings and he took them all under his wing. His heart of gold was always there to meet the challenge and when their pensions fell short of the rent, gentleman Karim bore the expense from his own pocket. Tears run down my cheeks as I recall his generosity, revealed to me by Ann Nduki after she took the job at Plums; he was seeking an Assistant Manager at the time and Ann filled the position after leaving the charity Barnado's. My excommunity development friend Gerry Farrell from Machakos, was by then the General Manager at Barnado's, with his dear wife Margot making all the decisions, though Gerry on paper was running the show. The Farrells had twins in the family and 5 children in all; today the children are in their fifties and we still exchange greetings. Tony, one of their boys, now sports a dapper beard and runs a safari outfit in Karen supported by Liz; the lovely lady from Denmark whom I first met at Barnado's when they were courting, 'sweet sixteen' and all that.

There were many good men in the Provincial Administration and because of their goodness they were never remembered. It was always the crooks that surfaced to occupy the limelight, and nothing was ever going to change. However, new adventures in Nairobi lay ahead and I was eager to start on the annual estimates for the Ministry of Lands and Settlement. My portfolio was serious businesss and lots of money was on the table; how to get it into our ministry pocket's was my challenge. The tug of war between the extravagant, that's us, and the meany, the Treasury, usually left us the loser with only a small compromise to maintain public relations. In the first place departmental estimates were presented to the Ministry for compilation against the money likely to be available, which also included British-aid money tied to British goods; such as Land Rovers, Ford Cars, Morris and Austin Trucks. BP and Shell petrol was also included to make up the numbers. After which we were almost home and dry. The estimates required approval by parliament following debate, and our minister presented the figures with explanatory notes that I had supplied; a challenge I relished, describes it well.

I would trim the departmental demands within our ministry, since I knew what the Treasury was offering. The Treasury would then become the meany and trim my demands even further. The rule of thumb was to over-claim in the first place and treasury knew it, so they automatically made some cuts as part of the bigger game. My opposite number in the treasury was Chris Kahara, a cheerful tight-fisted guy born in the shadows of Mount Kenya; we always had a great rapport when the snows were fresh and crispy years ago. The Kenya Pipeline was his final fiefdom many years hence, and it came complete with a company helicopter to keep his golfing dates.

Some people had all the luck, and some people didn't like it! But Chris's real good fortune in my eyes was an XK Jaguar he left behind as an epitaph, when he passed on. Its beauty was matched by his husky voice, resonating wit and humour. Philip Ndegwa was in league with Chris during budget time, but usually left him to his own devices that never seemed to match mine. Like 'Oliver Twist', we always wanted more. Large supplementaries were practically unheard of, and much to his credit Chris was equally fair with all the ministries and you overspent at your peril. How times have changed in 50 years; stringent accounting is now old-fashioned, and no longer do accounting officers pay token amounts or anything else from their own pockets to cover over-expenditure. And there were no luxury red-leather seats to pamper honourable backsides; you got a wooden chair with arms, government issue; grin and bear it was the rule. Not even Mzee Kenyatta's first cabinet chair was any different from the standard government issue, other than the national coat of arms on the red plastic back support. Our government office carpets covered small patches of naked floor, ten by twelve feet and not an inch more. Red for the Minister, blue for the PS was the rule, and when my luck was in, I managed with a piece of coconut matting.

21

Anecdotes have always been part of Kenyan society, and Mzee Pembe was an adorable comic in the sixties. He expounded funny scenes and made the masses laugh in those far off days. Unfortunately, his humour was often beyond my understanding, so I'll throw myself upon your good nature to enjoy a couple of personal stories, I claim to know something about.

Parliament, without doubt, was the most exciting aspect of all my duties during the whole of my 13 years in government service. Manipulations from the destitute to the elite in the ministry tended to blow the mind away, encourage sleepless nights, and even after a lapse of years flash-backs can be entertaining. It was Henry Kuria and Ralph Palmer, the assistant secretaries, who had the job of informing the minister about his response to parliamentary questions. That was after many in the ministry had added their two-cents of information to the package. We were in the mid 1960s, and at that time the very existence of the Ministry of Lands and Settlement was like a red rag to a bull, emulating on a less stringent scale to the Europeans who took 'vacant' land in the 1920s. The new panic actually started around '63, and without exception every

Kenyan was drooling over a 'slice of the cake' for personal profit. All, without exception, wanted title to a piece of the country. Avariciousness, extreme greed, is the words I'll use to describe the lust for land, though they only scratched the surface. Imagine if you can, all catagories of land were under seige; the bigger the portion grabbed the tastier it got, and the more the grabber wanted 'to eat'. At the dawn of independence, there was enough unallocated government land for all Kenyans to benefit from a few acres, but in real life there wasn't enough to go around. Masafaras, the ordinary wananchi, could only offer a prayer to fulfil their wishes, and it usually went unanswered. By now, the European land-grabbers from the past were primitive history overnight; a new and more adept elite had taken over. But land was not the only target of the grabbers; thousands of government houses countrywide had also been acquired to produce another headache for the anti-corruption teams. In this case, the 'county eaters' who missed the deal could help with envy as their motive, if they weren't too full of wind. Much like the cows in the fields accused of aiding climate change by the recent UN jolly in Gigiri, who themselves left behind much carbon from the rich Kenyan food, as they blew their last on the airport road in hundreds of cars and diesel buses.

Parliamentary questions were regularly passed onto Henry and I, with instructions to find the answers for our bosses. The Minister would then change the wording to suit his mood and the time allowed within the session. Finance was another key ministry and the next most important to Lands. After all, money oiled the wheels of government and without allowances nothing was going to move. Supply and demand was the name of the game, and it was Chris Kahara's turn to scratch his head when James Gichuru received financial questions from the legislature, which kept him busy with less time to question us about our annual estimates; one of his other duties.

We never received the questions directly, the route was 'scenic' via the Speaker who passed them to our Minister. He would then discuss their delicacy with Peter Shiyukah, who would in turn pass them over to us with the Minister's directions as to how they should be dealt with. We then took the initiative like all well behaved civil servants, who ruled the country as directed by the PS, for the Minister to read out our brief designed to curb supplementaries. The initial reply was never the problem, it was the supplementary from the initial reply that usually gave cause for a lengthy debate. Sometimes we forecast the answers to a supplementary spot on, but if we didn't get it right the Minister was obliged to come up with the answer on a nominated day the following week. It was just one of the reasons why Henry and I spent so much time in the house at question time, 2.30 to 3.30 pm, the same as today. In addition, we were awed by the entertainment and the actors never failed to disappoint. MPs were born to perform and question time presented a stage to expand their egoes; the tabloids rarely failed to report.

Kenya has always been blessed with a super class of civil servant to run the country rather smoothly; they also left a few decisions for the politicians to get the credit. It was important for the politicians to get the feeling they were doing a good job in their transient positions, as the 'mandarins' played subtle games on their behalf. And when the Press gave credit to an elected member, none doubted the system was working well.

The words of wisdom crafted across the entrance to the august Chamber are… 'For the Welfare of Society and the Just Government of Men.' You can bet your life the women are working on changing these words to suit their new thinking; how to muscle-in on leadership skills, an item long long overdue. The pinching of bottoms 'Italian style', verbal endearment, wicked language or brushing past a hallowed figure in the packed SGR train is no longer fun; it could leathal when the 'snakes' rattle their tails, and shout rape 20 years later. '*Me-too*', has suddenly become a 'war-cry', the fun in life has disappeared and rightly so; men are now on notice and must mind their manners and keep their hands to themselves. There's a lesson to learn from a world gone mad, where the 'me too' black dress is symbolic. Mouth to mouth resuscitation is now too hot handle, so relax and let the body breath its last or face the music on survival.

The Speaker of the National Assembly was Humphrey Slade supported by his deputy Fitz de Souza, and the civil servants' benches were on their either side. As the proceedings progressed, those manly words "For the Welfare of Society" were spread across the chamber entrance to look us straight in the eye, as the dignity of the house relied on those who passed there under. The Speaker used a black Mercedes with a newly invented registration, SNA 1 as of today, and his deputy owned a 'banger' to get around. No chase-cars were involved; pomp and pageant was at a minimum to save the taxpayer's money. Ministers were responsible people; Kenyatta was king and the Finance Minister James Gichuru, who stood-in for him when he wasn't around in the '61 elections, was morally his second-in-command. He could bank on Kenyatta's backing from the 'old guard' days; when they stood together and none got in their way. But with the 2010 constitution, the Speaker is now third in line should the President die in office; God forbid. So the more chase-cars in the chase, the safer we should feel.

To watch a parliamentary session at question time from the civil servants benches next to the Speaker was a privilege almost beyond belief, and an honour bestowed on only a few. Henry and Ralph were usually there by themselves enjoying the entertainment. The 2nd Kenya parliament was in session as I slipped through the heavily padded door prodded by Henry; the MPs were debating issues of national importance. If I was asked to comment upon the scene, I would liken their activities to a formal family gathering with common sense and a sprinkling of humour to drive them forward; they were lovely people. Naturally, some members had their moments and were ruffled on occasions by lively debate, much to the enjoyment of the whole chamber. The leaders in the earlier parliaments had yet to swell their allowances and the ordinary citizen approved of their earnings. There was only one lively sitting that I know of, when the Parliamentary Mace was dropped on the floor by an angry member, who was duly admonished and chucked out of the chamber, matter closed. There was no TV for the public to examine the spots on MPs' faces, or even mine for that matter, so we posed in a more natural manner with spots and all for the exclusive pleasure of our closest neighbours. Personal humour was usually to the fore when raising a point of order, and when replying to a question, a subtle innuendo could pose an extra question in return.

Martin Shikuku, the darling of the House and a favourite entertainer, wore a red bow-tie at question time that attracted an immediate point of order about the member's dress. For once the Speaker ruled the frivolous point to be valid, and much to the delight of the sitting members Shikuku was ejected from the Chamber. But much to his credit, his high spirits never let him down and he came back fighting the very next day; he had spotted a back-bencher on the opposite side of the house in suspicious dress mode. In fact, he could hardly contain himself before question time began, and for those who knew him well something was up as he bounced around about to explode; his jumpy movements made everyone nervous and gave him away. True to form, he was on his feet within seconds of question time starting.

"Mr Speaker, Sir, on a point of order?" Shikuku kept his arm in the air to assert his presence, and bent his hand with a pointed finger in a particular direction.

"Can you confirm that the honourable member for East Pokot has been disinfested before he entered this chamber?"

All eyes then followed the pointed finger and some members stood up to get a better view of the man from East Pokot dressed in a Colobus monkey skin; an ostrich-feather vein reaching over the top of his head waved a ball of rabbit's fur to complete his outfit. A wicked glee then resonated throughout the chamber.

"Order! Order! Order!" Humphrey Slade imposed his presence. And no sooner had Members sat down from viewing the perfectly acceptable tribal-dress, another commotion errupted when their unified weight caused the older benches to collapse. By the end of the session all present had had a jolly good time, after which they settled down to serious business.

Sometimes, when Tom Mboya, Mwai Kibaki, James Gichuru, Double 'O' as Jaramogi was called, and heckler Martin Shikuku were present, the show was electric and humour flowed with points of order; genuine and non genuine. The idea was to lodge a 'spanner in the works' or perhaps some 'soothing ointment' to get the House business done. It depended on the forces for or against on the day, as changeable as the weather.

Tom Mboya and Martin Shikuku were famous for their humourous repartee, and on occasion the member for Butere 'She kuku', jokingly translated as 'Hen', became the butt of Tom's attention with a point of order.

"Mr Speaker, Sir?" Tom was on his feet, "can you please confirm the honourable member for Butere has a fire in his trousers, he can't seem to sit down?" The house erupted in laughter as Tom scored a point in his favour.

"Order! Order!" Fitz de Souza was not amused. "Next question?" During another afternoon session, a motion was proposed to ban women from wearing trousers in government offices. They were called 'trousers' in those days; women's jeans, tights, leggings and bikers as we know them now, were not yet chique modern fashions.

Even, to quote my own mother: a woman in trousers wearing high heels creates a sensuous scene, which is enough to encourage loose morals and seedy thoughts. But whatever the argument, and no mattter how old fashioned it was, morals in the 60s were still rather strict in spite of the avant-garde, dying to display their beauty. Shapely figures had always been there; but the fashion to show off the alluring to satisfy masculine minds had yet to arrive. Changing designs would eventually dictate the future, and some of the more trendy were making a name for themselves, but 'stretch-jeans' and 'skinnies' had yet to shine. To hide the sensuous at this late stage was tantamount to avoiding the facts; the genie was already out of the bottle and flauting desire. How such a motion had been raised in the august chamber left members searching for answers, but the rumour going the rounds was that of an amorous individual who had failed to concentrate in office time, when some girl's hips were wagging. Whatever the proposer of the motion had in mind is for your imagination; I'm only the one relaying the news as witnessed by me in the august chamber! These were only theories put forward by some deep thinking MPs, but it fell to the Attorney General to win the day if nothing was to change. The women were also determined to continue their open life-style, much to the delight of the *me-too* men. For us observers on the spot, the wearing of tight trousers debate was the ice cream on the apple pie for that particular session. We were enjoying our space next to the Speaker.

Charles Njonjo, the Attorney General, stood up to reply to the motion. He cast aside the written answer he was expected to read, since he knew exactly how to tackle the problem. With a confident expression on his face and a thumb tucked into his waistcoat pocket, he began his defence on behalf of the women. Noticeably so, he was also trying to hide a wry smile that reflected an inbuilt sense of humour shared by the majority in the house. A deathly silence then prevailed as the members strained to hear his answer; how to stick-up for the rights of women. What happened and who won the day rested with 'Sir Charles' entirely; he spoke for the government and the rights of women to wear clothes of their choosing. The jealous wives and the wandering eyes of their husbands had put them up to this prank, and it had to be a prank when no supplementary was raised. The debate was lively and good-humoured, but not too laughable for some with pressure in the bedroom hanging over their heads. The proposer openly admitted his flesh to be as weak as the next, but then conceded he'd got a lot older and gone off the boil; he hoped his wife was listening. Much laughter followed and the chamber was happy. Sir Charles then declared there was nothing wrong with some quality cloth on a quality base; one was free to look and not touch, or look the other way. The motion subsequently failed.

Congratulations Sir Charles, 99 today I hear, and may God bless you with many more to come. A Twitter from the Queen is due next year, but in the meantime Philip has a brand new Range Rover and he's only 97, why not join him for a spin in Windsor Park?

22

The previous week had been more busy than usual; the brighteyed re-energised MPs were back from recess with ready questions to be raised about land. And as usual, no stone would be left unturned, but in the end no stone was touched, and the lie of the land remained the same. MPs were always enthusiastic during the first few weeks of the new parliament, when attendance allowances amounted to immediate cash as their points of order ran out of steam drowned by the more weighty matters of state. In the 60s, MPs were paid moderate salaries and not called 'MPigs' like they are today. Even the seating in the House was a palatable cream leather bench similar to the green ones in the House of Commons in London; mindful of the cost to their hungry voters. In those far off days nothing was billions of shillings for thieves to short supply or up contract prices; red leather to cosset an honourable buttock then remained a future red leather experience yet to be eased upon, with a heave and a sigh to express relaxation. Everything was still low key and didn't have to be the best in the world for the 'selfless' servants of the people, who according to some were about to court beggar status in 2017.

That's if their present salaries are cut by $900 to a mere $6000 per month with millions of shillings in gifted cars and mileage claims at ten times the national average monthly wage. House mortgages and rent-free accommodation has just been added to the package. Their bundles at the end of the month to compensate for their toil and sweat, are some of the highest in the world. On the plus side for the ordinary people, freedom of the press has now come of age to be enjoyed by all Kenyans. Cartoons touch on the brilliant and tickle the inner mind to put smiles on faces; their easy humour is in a class of its own and loved by all who view it.

The Chairman was called the 'Chairman' of the PAC (Public Accounts Committee) in days of old, and was by tradition the leader of the opposition. It therefore followed that Jaramogi Oginga Odinga of the Kenya Peoples Union was the chairman when our ministry was summoned to appear before him. His seat in parliament was clearly defined to the left of the speaker with the likes of Achieng Oneko and Paul Ngei, to mention a few of his heavy weight colleagues.

That's how I found myself being questioned by double 'O' at the PAC. Shiyukah had given me the auditor's file to study ahead of time, for answers to roll off my tounge when Jaramogi began the questioning. The file outlined some of our more miserable accounting sins over the past 12 months, but nothing therein was likely to bring the government down. Peter was bound to attend as Permanent Secretary and Accounting Officer, since he was the one being threatened with a surcharge should his ministry have caused the exchequer a loss; a derisory thought in 2019. So whatever happened in the 60s on Shiyukah's watch was his responsibility, he was the one to be admonished by Odinga. In reality, it depended on how Jaramogi had woken up on that particular morning; Peter was his friend of years and Jaramogi was never one to punish friends because of his differences with Kenyatta. In fact, it had been some time since an accounting officer had been surcharged from any angle, but the opposition could be looking to score a point; one never knew.

The meeting was scheduled at a civilised hour, 10 am in the Commonwealth room on the 1st floor of the National Assembly; an elegant stairway leading up to this special room was our pleasure to grace. For me, it had been a simple matter of studying the files and presenting my person at the appointed hour. Peter and I would make our separate ways to the meeting, and the assumption was, little could go wrong.

9.30 am and I was on my way wearing my 'Sunday best'. I took the Silo Park lift at the back of the building with the usual squash of people, some of whom were travelling in a lift for the very first time in their lives; security was nil and rides were for free, so why not experience the up and down thrill if you came from upcountry. I suspect the lift stopped between the 5th and 6th floors; the emergency alarm was ringing and time aplenty was taken to respond to our plight. Nervous passengers even began to smoke before I told them to, 'put it out'. Some time elapsed and the doors eventually slid open; my tension then half disappeared as I panicked over to parliament. Entering the Commonwealth room for the very first time was a special experience for me, and as word of my lift debacle had already preceded my arrival the Chairman seemed in tolerant mood.

The Honourable Jaramogi Oginga Odinga greeted me from where he was seated across the Commonwealth table; he pointed to an empty chair, the only one vacant. The circular table in itself was a masterpiece of craftsmanship promoting

Commonwealth timbers; it was about 20 feet in diameter. The top was supported by a single row of inner legs leaving the outer circumference free standing; the surrounding chairs with wood-carved arms and back rests were heavily upholstered. Carafes of tap water with glasses on trays were interspersed at intervals around the table; special bottled water for newly sanitised stomachs was far too expensive, and multi-million flower displays were nowhere in sight. The wood panelled walls, rich in hue, have since been covered with filing cabinets and office junk if the latest TV scenes are true, but these features in their time were outstandingly beautiful when I first saw them. Mandazi and mixed tea are well liked today and speak of an unusual change to frugality, compared to the creamcake binges of yesteryear.

"Mr Palmer, I hear you've been stuck in the lift at the Silo Park," were Odinga's opening words. "So we'll have a coffee break now, for you to recover from your attempt to disappear.." He was in good form and those present laughed, myself included. He signalled the waiter with a motion of his hand for the feast to begin.

"Thank you Mr Chairman," what more could I say, discretion was sought and mistaken facetiousness was the last thing needed to carry the day.

A magical experience is about to begin, to mark my first and last time in the Commonwealth room. Waiters appeared in pristine white jackets fastened with shiny brass buttons up to the neck; similar to those I had last glimpsed on the Mombasa train many years in the past. They bore silver trays of fancy cream cakes and asked confirmation of your selection by pointing the tongs for your final approval; then to your delight, they lifted a piece of pastry onto your plate for the gastric juices to flow. On your right, a second waiter offered coffee from a silver coffee pot and matching milk jug. All told, this utopian existence lasted for about 30 minutes before we got down to serious business. The most glaring faux-pas stood out a mile and there was no doubt about it, our Minister had been badly advised. Peter in response, used some psychology and took a lashing from Jaramogi to give him the satisfaction of nailing the obvious to seize his 'pound of flesh'. The Transport Capital Vote had been debited with the cost of a Humber Super Snipe saloon, far above the Minister's entitlement; remember, this is in the 1960s and the public still came first.

Odinga then proved his understanding of our short comings by enumerating a list we didn't need him to recall; he clearly knew of the detail just like us; he talked absolute sense. By then, Peter was sufficiently energised to point out our 'saving grace'; ten thousand pounds was our surplus at the end of the financial year with a budget allocation of almost £6 million. True, there had been some last minute expenditure to use up unspent balances, blamed on the nasty habit of treasury making cuts the following year if you went 'to bed' with a large surplus. Unusual perhaps, but we were back in the 1960s and no cash had been stolen to appoint a commission to get to the bottom of anything, whilst enjoying the perks. And whilst on the subject of commissions, the size of members bottoms had nothing to do with their tasks, though they could have been quite large from sitting around doing nothing; since nothing ever seemed to happen.

Back in the office we breathed a sigh of relief and praised the high standard of the Commonwealth cakes. The small surcharge of £400 to give satisfaction to the chairman was nothing, compared to the quality of the vehicle the minister was now bound to own. The PS had been instructed to make deductions from Angaine's salary; £3400 per annum was the figure in those days, and from my personal knowledge the car was worth every penny. I think this was one of the few years that Jaramogi headed the Public Accounts Committee, though I know not for certain other than this year summons. It was Government policy to examine a cross-section of several ministries every year, and the Public Accounts Committee picked from a collection of auditor's reports where financial errors were highlighted. You had to take your turn like everyone else for coffee and cakes; a life changing experience, if you got lucky.

The City Hall that staged the Independence Ball in '63, was still the largest venue in town. The 34-floor Kenyatta Conference Centre engineered by the Israelis had yet to be built in 1974. So the old hall with a history was booked to launch the brainchild of Peter Shiyukah. The Kenya African Rally Drivers Club, designed to promote African participation in the East African Safari rally. This international rally, held over the Easter holidays, was the only time of the year when competitors drove like mad and legally broke all the traffic rules; the large numbers on their car doors appeared to inspire their madness. I reflected on my own efforts in the minister's Super Snipe when I attempted to reach 100 mph, and how science has lightened the machinery that held me back in those days. That Humber car, built like a 'bedstead', was never made to travel at speed, but now we're in the age of aluminium and Formula 1.

Peter Shiyukah and Tom Mboya had compatible humour and shared many a knowing laugh with their innuendo annoying those not on their higher-thinking plane. That's how they were and nothing was simplified to accommodate the less sensitive characters outside their circle. As it so happened, Peter and Tom had just returned from London before this African Rally Drivers launch at City Hall. And it came as no surprise to hear that the delegation had returned with juicy problems for the auditors at the end of the year. But in the meantime, some light relief was at hand as stories surfaced to entertain for weeks to come. Keeping a chauffeur idling outside the Hilton Hotel for 7 hours whilst they slept off their exhaustion from the flight had cost over a £100, and was not the most expedient thing to do.

The Hilton Hotel Park Lane at £9 a night had also presented a bit of a challenge to the guests from Kenya, when their shoes for polishing were placed outside their doors at night, only to be found missing in the morning. Miraculously, they then reappeared after directions from the front desk. A hole in the wall was specially designed, to shoot cleaned shoes directly into their wardrobes. But well before then the delegation had strutted around in the hallway, debating the issue; each had only one pair of shoes. According to Shiyukah, a few had holes in their socks, and the ministers being the biggest brass had bigger holes than anyone else. Much joking followed that same evening over a drink when the morning drama was replayed by some of the best actors in the group, in exaggerated form of course.

To launch the Kenya African Rally Drivers Club an inauguration speech from a patron was needed, and Tom Mboya was willing to fulfil both duties, which left me to outline his speech. He then told me he didn't really need any speech at all.

"Just give me three sentences about the club and I'll do the rest," were his words exactly. And from thereon he talked about the challenge to the up and coming African drivers, with their needs for financial support if they were to succeed. Safari was an expensive business and Joginder the flying Sikh, with his driving skills then led the local pack, much aided by his hard-earned sponsor-ships, as a winner on a regular basis.

"Why were the local Africans nowhere in sight?" Tom asked the question and declared the answer at the same time, "the enormous expense involved." The Swedes who often won, had hands-on factory support. Vic Preston and Bill Parkinson with their Shell service station on University Way used a lot of their own money to wave the Kenyan flag; natural talent and their own resources achieved success. I know for a fact that Vic Preston was more than generous with his support for Peter, even then no member of the Club ever made the grade. Partaking rather than winning was the thrill! Peter used an Alfa Romeo and Triumph 2000 in his time, and the seat backs were flattened when he took off; power was not in contention. Unfortunately, perseverance to practice combined with his senior government job was not an ideal platform; so nothing ever came of his brilliant idea to found the Rally Driver's Club. Peter's spirit was in overdrive during his two attempts and taking part was his prize, but to win was a bonus he never expected.

***

Some events that occurred during my government service appear amusing and worthy mention, though they're unlikely to ruffle your feathers, nor give you sleepless nights. I merely recount some of these happenings to titillate your curiosity Kenya style, so if you're now on the 'hook' don't wriggle, lie back and relax, let me reel you in.

Something was in full swing in Mombasa and the presence of the ministry was required. There was a definite reason why we were there; the Agricultural Show was underway and fortunately for us we had a friend in town, Shariff Nassir was his name. He was courting a certain lady at the time and a low profile liaison was preferable for him, which led to our introduction to the Port Reitz Hotel on the way to the Airport by the same name; yet to be renamed Moi International.

The Port Reitz Hotel was an ancient colonial relic with a glamorous past. It was named after a certain Royal Navy Lieutenant J.J. Reitz, the first 'Mombasa Resident' in 1824, and for all we knew these same stone walls and the solid timber doors had been touched by Reitz some two hundred years before. The verandah on which we took our drinks had a modern terrazzo floor, but had you troubled to raise your butt from the wicker chair to peep over the parapet, the harbour lights on rippling waters were mightily impressive. However, our company seated on the wicker chairs neither raised their butts nor did any peeping; a White Cap beer was upper most in their minds and such mundane activities as looking around was for the tourists, of which I was the only one. For a change, no one was unduly worried about who would pickup the bill for drinks and bitings, Nassir had invited and Nassir would pay; it suited him to impress his young ladies. As a powerful businessman in his own right with his future position as Assistant Minister for Commerce still in waiting, he remained a big commercial-wheel and special friend to Jesse Gachago.

My room was in the same block as Jesse's at the Nyali Beach Hotel. James Maina was independent and so was Peter. But when at leisure (see photo) they usually had drinks on the verandah of my Nyali Beach cottage, where I would exercise my newly found training from Peter; how to avoid a pile of bills when these fellows were earning more than I was. "Keep an eye on things, be vigilant", Peter would say, "or you may end up with a terrible shock when checking out." Somehow, the belief that the white man was rich was still lingering on and the fallacy was taking too long to die. Cash was king in those days, and credit cards belonged to the Yanks.

Doonholm Stadium on Doonholm road Nairobi, was the equivalent to Wembley Stadium, Wembley Park London; each promoted football in their country of choice. Besides watching the matches in Nairobi, the heads of government would enjoy the crowds and live off the results after the game with a bottle in hand well into the night. According to Peter Anyumba, Director of Surveys and later an MP in life, a well behaved crowd was the key to enjoyment, and Shiyukah also agreed, they made the event attractive. So with all anxiety put aside we set off for the venue in two separate cars. Anyumba would take his own, and I would get a lift with Peter in his safari-tuned Alfa Romeo; naturally, at breakneck speed. All three of us were looking forward to an enjoyable afternoon and the tickets would be purchased at the gate, no sweat involved.

Government office times had yet to change to a 5-day week, so we worked from 8 am to 4.30 pm with an hour for lunch throughout the week; Saturday until 12.30 pm. Anyumba's offices were a collection of wooden buildings halfway across town in the vicinity of Kingsway Police Station; reason enough to meet at the stadium. His offices were also noted for their shabbiness in creosoted colonial timbers, similar in age to CID headquarters in Uhuru Park, eventually replaced by the Serena

Hotel to yield unrivalled views of the city skyline.

We left our offices midday Saturday, for the scheduled kick-off at 3 pm. A couple of famous teams were about to do battle at Doonholm Stadium, and a rough energetic match was expected. These guys tended to kick the hell out of each other, so the stage was set and expectations were high for Gor-Mahia and Nakuru All-Stars to explode! Wise to the fact that their football techniques were far from refined, we were looking forward to a match with the usual shouting and jeering. As spectators from our VIP seats we were able to weigh every detail and enjoy every minute as the afternoon loomed large, anticipation was in the air. The kick-off went according to plan and the first half ended goalless. One player had been sent off and another was changed; the game was proceeding in a more orderly manner than anyone expected. At the interval we bought Coke in a glass bottle before the second half began; plastic bottles for water or Coke had still to be developed and glass had yet to be banned from match venues. A sharp shrill singular note from the referee's whistle got the second half underway. An offside goal was then disallowed, and to compound the referee's poor decision, a free kick scored a few minutes later against the team with the disallowed goal. The whole match then exploded and bottles began to fly onto the pitch, before they changed direction into the stands of the opposing supporters. I was never that brave to face rioting crowds and neither was Anyumba, so he led the way climbing over a barbed wire fence with his lanky legs. Peter quickly followed with a spring in his steps, and I the not so nimble tagged along in the rear. Surprise, surprise, the riot police were already on the spot to soften up the crowd before they got down to business in earnest, as they upped the rhythm so to speak. I came to know later that a contingent of police was always on hand just in case. And had I known in advance, I would have let the other two enjoy the rioting on their own.

The white tear gas smoke searched every nook and cranny, but the experienced Anyumba knew exactly what to do; he grabbed my arm and led the way to the outside ticket office, where by luck, the door was open. Once inside, we locked ourselves in and sat under the table clasping our knees, waiting for the gas to blow-over and tempers to cool. Why, and I still repeat the same question today, did the police break the window and drop a teargas bomb into our hiding place; fortunately it fell into a tin being used for rubbish but the question still remained, why do such a thing in the first place? We were out of there in double quick time and the police when they saw us were sorry, but by then we didn't want to hear any regrets as we took off on foot leaving our cars facing the stadium wall. Cars parked at the stadium were few and always safe according to Anyumba. Sunday morning I was with Peter to collect our car and conclude my first and last football match in Nairobi; interesting maybe, but definitely not my cup of tea!

Around this time parking boys were many and the new parking meters had arrived to relieve unemployment, so like it or not, a new cadre of parking attendants were now gracing the new city scene. Legitimate charges were 50 cts for 1 hour and Sh.1 for 2 hours; the pointer in the meter buzzed a little longer if you chose the 2 hour shift. Alternatively, if you engaged a 'parking engineer' who had mastered his trade, it would cost Shs.2 for a whole day. A wire coat-hanger was his tool and the hook-part worked wonders. Things came to life when the wire was forced into the slot, and the next thing you knew the meter was charged. These little 'devils' also used the same technique to force your car door and steal your radio, so a certain amount of soul-searching was always present when you employed a crook, to 'crook' the City Council. But those guilty thoughts soon disappeared, when the City towed off your car for practically no reason at all.

The nightclub scene was preferable to a football match and more my idea of entertainment. And believe you me, the International Casino on Ainsworth Road close to the national museum was the biggest and the best in town. The click click of the little white ball bouncing on the roulette wheel brings back the suspense, a moment before the croupier grabs your chips. Run by Italians in a professional manner, croupiers wore tuxedos, dress mattered in those days. Patchy-arsed-freaks in torn jeans were blocked at the door; the sweet scented only were welcome, much to the delight of those not yet not in the gutter. World famous acts were part of the scene, embracing the high-kicking Tiller Girls and their razzmatazz when they stopped over on their worldwide tours. New York, Las Vegas, Sydney and Nairobi, was their route in the 60s. Nakedness on the stage in Africa at that time remained a risky business, and wine on occasion was served in tea pots, not to offend the religious.

The new Bacchus Club in the 80s was another hive of activity that attracted quality stars; those who had performed at the New Stanley Grill before it was redesigned as a private club. The covered grotto approach from Standard Street offered the prospect of an adventurous evening, with a lively band and world famous artists. The man with the gift to launch this special place was Alan Doig, who parked his golden Mercedes sports in the basement of the Standard Bank building at the end of the street. Sadly, Alan the charismatic with good ideas, shot himself dead in dramatic style for reasons best known to him. He caused a lot of grief for those who knew him well and in particular, to his associate Robbie Armstrong of distant 'Starlight' fame, whose wife Jean owned Jean's Bar in Nairobi West. By reputation, Robbie's Starlight Club was the place to be when you were on the razzle, but in the present day, the site on consecrated land is occupied by the Integrity Centre.

Rumour has it, and it might be true, there are evil vibes on that particular plot where people fear to tread, and many a spirit has haunted those who've conducted business there. After the demise of the Starlight, the Trade Bank continued the rot, and the present day tenants are struggling to overpower the 'integrity ghost'. A change of the guard at the ill-named centre is a regular feature, and if honest staff get too close to solving a crime they're obliged to tread with caution. The plan has always been to set a snail to catch a cheetah, but to choose an athletic snail is not the intention. The jailing of a chicken thief, when the rouges running government are out and about makes little sense, but that's how the system justifies redemption. The fat-cats are getting fatter, and the court cases are left to gather dust; the integrity ghost looks on and laughs, but he can't laugh himself to death, he died long ago.

In its day the 'Starlight' had a reputation that ventured on the daring; it was reputed to trick foreign visitors into believing they'd lived life on the brink in darkest Africa, after only a minute in the entrance. How wrong they were, but the folks back home who didn't know any better were forced to hear of their risky business over and over again. When the TV cameras chose to cross the threshold of an evening, much covering of faces would follow and mistaken identity was pleaded by many a family man, said to be somewhere else before he left home.

Let's now move back to the early 60s and 70s and examine some of the more intimate clubs; the Equator, Hallians, and the Sal Davis Night Club, to touch on a few of the more famous, I'm qualified to recall. The Equator Club was best known for the Hollywood Stars who had made such epic films as 'The Snows of Kilimanjaro'. It was located on the first floor where the IPS building now stands, adjacent to the New Stanley hotel. Though some of the stars preferred to retire to the quiet of the Norfolk, or perhaps the Brackenhurst far out of town, much favoured by Robert Mitchum. The Equator Club subsequently moved to the building opposite the Khoja Mosque in Government Road (Moi Avenue). I couldn't afford to be a regular at any of these establishments, though I did enjoy them when I had the means. On occasion, I rubbed shoulders with the likes of Miriam Makeba and Dorothy Masuka, and Lord Bryner the Calypso King from Trinidad; all performers of their times.

Sal Davis, I claim to be a distant friend of mine, but a greater friend of his was Sammy Lui the TV announcer. Sal never lacked a place to sing with a stage all of his own; the Sal Davis Night Club in Koinange Street. The mushroom shape at the Caltex station was the place to be of an evening if you wanted to hear 'Unchain My Heart', his regular signature tune. His husky voice would make the ladies swoon in Nairobi, if he wasn't wooing them in Dubai.

Hallian's Club in Victoria Street (Tom Mboya) and Mr Hirji the owner, were equally popular names around town. Fadhili

Williams the musical genius with his abundant grey hair at the time, was a regular visitor to Hallians. Peter Shiyukah first introduced me to this talented composer, who was made more popular by Miriam Makeba when she stayed in the States to rail against apartheid. "Malaika, Nakupenda Malaika." Angel, I love you my angel was first recorded in 1961, and became one of her favourite repertoire tunes.

It was a bright sunny day and spirits were high as we waited for the lift at the rear of the Silo Park building; the Law Courts hadn't moved an inch and the Re-insurance Plaza was still in place; Koinange's parking lot, gifted by his friend Kenyatta, was bare and bleak as usual.

"Ralph, come here a minute?" Shiyukah called me over while the lift was taking its time to arrive.

"Tell me?" I asked, as I joined him at the window.

"See that tree stump…?" he pointed towards Koinange's plot.

"Where?" I couldn't see any particular tree stump.

"Down there, near that big eucalyptus; the biggest tree on the plot."

"Is it yours?" I was trying to be difficult.

"No; it's not mine exclusively," he laughed, "but I was sitting on it earlier this morning and what do you think happened?"

Peter wanted to make his story interesting to exercise his usual humour. A tree stump under a tree and my boss was sitting on it earlier in the day; surely I had to ask him why he was sitting on such a stump.

"Ok, I know you want me to ask you why? So now, I'm asking you why?" I knew Peter well.

"Have you noticed my hair?"

"Well, it looks half-cut to me?"

"Exactly; so now you can see how difficult life is for a PS when even his barber is chased away while performing his skills. Just imagine, a senior civil servant guiding the interests of the nation and his barber suddenly takes-off whilst cutting my hair. You know we Africans have many uses for trees besides charcoal and building. For instance, we can use a twig from a branch to clean our teeth, we can fall sleep under a shady one, and it also doubles as a mirror-hanger when we have our hair cut. Now hear this; I was sat on that stump down there in old Koinange's plot using the haircut mirror activity on the tree, and all I wanted was the skills of a traditional barber; and that's when my problem rears its ugly head." Peter was by now enjoying the drama created during his exposition.

"So you see, I'm seated down there and we agree on the price for him to produce his clippers and comb. First off, he takes a big breath and blows them clean for the exercise to get under way in a more 'hygienic' manner. Please note, spit and all that is part of the service and comes for free." Peter enjoyed my silence; his verbal intrigue had me hooked.

"Well, at first I'm keeping an eye on him through a piece of broken mirror balanced on a nail stuck in the tree trunk; then I close my eyes for one second only, as his cutting movement relaxes my head. Imagine, just one second. And the next thing I know is, I'm jerked awake by a City Council askari who has studied the quality of my suit and decided to treat me with care."

"You're not allowed to sit here, Sir," he declares. "Idling in this area is an offence; you'll have to come with me to be charged at City Hall."

"Eh! What type of idiot did he think I was? Ok, I know

he was only trying to do his job by interfering with members of the public, but I wasn't about to go anywhere with him and certainly not to City Hall. Imagine my position; the place where my classmate Isaac Lugonzo is the Mayor; he'd be telling a joke about me for the rest of his life. Anyway, the barber had certainly disappeared with his piece of broken mirror, so I brazened it out and gave the man 50 cts for a couple of mugs of tea." At that time the Daily Nation was 25 cts. Sh.60 today.

"And I'll tell you this; I won't be dozing off the next time I use that stump down there; I'll disappear with the barber, mirror and all." He made his point and laughed.

"Wow! Thanks for the tip," we were still laughing as the lift arrived. Peter always told a good story, with one hand close to his mouth directing his voice for your exclusive listening.

Toothbrushes, or mswaki in Swahili, have always contributed to the brilliant white teeth of the African fraternity before the white man's sweets crept into their diet. My informant tells me that they were on one of their London trips and staying at a WestEnd hotel when one of their team, a minister no less, decided to obtain a traditional toothbrush by climbing a tree early one morning in Oxford Street, near to Marble Arch. Ole, the big guy with the gleaming teeth and loops in his lobes got the blame, but was back in the hotel before a second witness could verify his antics. The question then begged; when did pastoralists learn to climb trees without a hungry lion in sight, food for thought, I do believe?

It was a Saturday morning and the town was fuller than usual; the busy and the idle were in equal numbers and a show outside the Standard Bank in Kenyatta Avenue was entertaining the long suffering public, bullied on occasion by the City Fathers. City life was a humdrum affair and little ever happened to lift the spirits of the citizens until this particular morning, when an impromptu show by a parking boy changed their gloom to laughter. For a change, a young boy had the edge over the city council inspectors and a growing crowd was enjoying the delight of the moment. So what was the attraction, and what had caused this little bit of light-relief just before the weekend?

You'll be the judge and this is the scene. The saga began when a city askari had a firm grip on a parking boy's ear, for his little friend to snatch the askari's hat to make him let go. The trick had worked and the askari did let go to retrieve his hat, but quick off the mark, the little fellow climbed the Askari Monument to escape his clutches. The heavy askari was then left scratching his head at the foot of the monument, with the little boy 30 feet high next to the askari statues. It was his time to shine and he knew it; the crowd was enjoying his performance and with his new hat he was saluting and bowing in response to their cheering. To restore the dignity of the council, back-up arrived and discussions took place for a ladder to appear. The little boy then threw the hat into crowd and slipped down the back of the monument; a happy ending was had by all. The council gave up the chase when the hat was recovered, and the miscreant took-off 'Kipchoge-style', to play another day.

Epilogue

As the title suggests, this book concentrates on the years 1955 to 1969, but sometimes reaches into the future or dips into the past to add pili pili, chili, to the detail. Future industry and full employment are top-of-the-pops in the 21st century. High fashion Kenya-style is leading the African continent; bright colours, super designs on beautiful ladies are flooding the runways and it appears the men have been left behind, but for those in the know, they are very much part of the talent behind the scenes.

Imagine, the year is 2035 and I'm long gone to wherever, I hope it's 'upstairs' but who knows? I've left you lucky people behind to fight amongst yourselves as you struggle against a plastic planet dispensing bottled water, and a national debt beyond belief. Nairobi continues to be the City in the Sun, in spite of its urban planning that fails to rock the super-power Kenya holds. A new parliament building is reconstructed in steel and glass, after a mysterious fire purged the rot, endemic in the old. The 'Disney World' recreation centre originally built for MPs to relax, is now a hospital for the benefit of the poor. Capital punishment exists for exceptional thieves, with the possibility of a life sentence in exchange for the return of all stolen assets. Mandatory 10-year sentences have been awarded by the African Union Court, newly appointed to replace the Kenyan judiciary, unwilling to prosecute their own. Something about living in 'glass-houses' and throwing stones finally forces the issue. A young coalition government in their mid-forties augurs well for the future; whilst divine intervention is praised for the new police uniforms produced in error without deep pockets.

Just to land at Jomo Kenyatta International Airport is a pleasure in itself; the reception staff are the best in the world according to the latest international polls. Synonymously, Kenya Airways, the Pride of Africa, operates a fleet of the latest jets. It has recently added the new supersonics from America, to allow a repeat of the Concorde genius decades ago. The 5 hour trip to Washington DC from Nairobi is working well, much to the chagrin of its competitors.

The feeder-road from JKIA sweeps into a clover-leaf-flyover that disperses traffic to different parts of the city; it also serves Mombasa in the East, Mount Kenya and the lakes to the North and West. Oil, bountiful oil, is flowing overseas from the Lamu delta network. Since the Mombasa refinery has never been repaired, the Nigerian system of re-importing refined oil is firmly in place. Seepage is high and points to a scam, and the usual platitude comes into play; such things happen all over the world, to make it okay in Kenya.

New infrastructures are racing ahead and the bandits in government are on the back foot. Development-aid and begging for loans is a thing of the past; Kenyans are justly proud of their third generation independence. A young Kalenjin rocket has cracked the 2hr marathon barrier by 50 seconds, 1hr 59.10 is the new world record. The semi-finals in the Africa Cup of Nations have been achieved and the championship is almost within their grasp.

A new suspension bridge, the longest in Africa, has replaced the Likoni ferry and property prices on the South Coast have moved to new highs. The subterranean rail, a cross between the

New York City Subway and the London Underground network, is a boon to the Nairobi commuters; it stretches as far as Thika and Konza Silicon Valley. Traffic jams are a thing of the past; matatu mounds of scrap have been recycled into microwave-ovens for the export market, and driverless buses at a shilling a ride have flooded the city. The narrow gauge rail, originally built for the gullible, has finally been stretched by 50 kilometres into the city centres of Nairobi and Mombasa. Kenyans are happy; the fast lane in life is open to the entrepreneur and they're enjoying the ride of their lives. However, the feet of modern man are still in mid-air with neither the patience of a Monk nor the wisdom of Solomon. A railway is built to end up nowhere (Suswa perhaps), and the super concrete highways that speed past village life are about to bury grandma's roots and customs cultivated over the years. Going back to the village to show off her grandchildren; those little adventurers, who love to climb trees and cuddle fluffy lambs, is about to become a rare treat.

The number of Kenya citizens of Chinese origin has increased dramatically, and their presence is considered a small price to pay for their expertise. Nevertheless, a watchful eye is monitoring the parallel between their influx and the coolies who built the first railway system never to return to India. Society still owes the Indian community a monstrous debt for their trading skills in that pioneering era. The new and less compassionate communists controlled by big brother in Beijing have now stepped into the Indian shoes; their future looks bright and they'll demand their pound of flesh, but who knows of their measure that originally shone like the star in the East. Poverty thrust upon Ecuador, Sri Lanka's 99-year harbour lease and an island in the Maldives is so far claimed to meet Chinese debts, and a new twist in the tale could be in the offing. But for the present, the cruel world out there remains a 'pussy-cat' in disguise.

The story...

The author regales us with an exciting journey into the past; you will witness momentous events that shaped Kenya's history; these were exhilarating times. You shall meet the pioneering personalities of a newly independent Kenya; those who helped to mould the country before and after independence. You will travel the path they took during the struggle from colonial rule to the raising of the Kenya flag. Districts mentioned in detail are Nyeri, Meru, Ukambani, Nakuru, Kitale, Turkana, Baringo, and the Capital City in the Sun.

Peter Shiyukah and the author, Lower Hill Road, Nairobi, 1966.

Destiny aggressively beckoned one bleak morning in London; the Daily Telegraph told of a job in Kenya. It was 1955 and the Colonies were still recruiting, Ralph Palmer became their man. Shortly after this, he landed at Eastleigh International Airport on his way to Nyeri, Central Province. A place of beauty, where the snows run deep on Mount Kenya and touch all those in its shadows. 'Rough Justice', one of his earlier books, was nominated to the Dublin Literary Awards in 2009.

Ralph Palmer, 2020

ISBN 000-0-0000-0000-0

www.ingramcontent.com/pod-product-compliance
Lightning Source LLC
Chambersburg PA
CBHW050740080526
44579CB00017B/73